Family Matters

Family Matters

A guide to healthier and happier relationships

Robin Skynner

Methuen

First published in Great Britain in 1995
by Methuen London
an imprint of Reed Books Ltd
Michelin House, 81 Fulham Road, London SW3 6RB
and Auckland, Melbourne, Singapore and Toronto

The bulk of the essays in this volume were originally published
in the *Guardian* under the title 'Home Front'. 'Family Therapist as
Family Scapegoat' was originally published in the *Journal of Family
Therapy* and 'A Recipe for Health and Happiness' in *She* magazine.

A CIP catalogue record for this book
is available at the British Library
ISBN 0 413 69600 6

Typeset by Deltatype Ltd, Ellesmere Port, Cheshire
Printed and bound in Great Britain
by Clays Ltd, St Ives PLC

Contents

Preface

*T*his book is the result of a series of articles I wrote for the *Guardian* newspaper between 1990 and 1993. I am grateful to the newspaper for their permission to reproduce them here, sometimes in their slightly extended original form. (Two other articles are included: 'Family Therapist as Family Scapegoat' was first published (in a substantially longer form) in the *Journal of Family Therapy* in 1979 and 'A Recipe for Health and Happiness' in *She* magazine in 1991.)

Those years were busy ones for me, not least because John Cleese and I were in the final stages of writing, then publishing, our *Life and How to Survive It*, the sequel to our *Families and How to Survive Them*, which is still going strong after its first appearance in 1983. Some of the areas we explored then, notably what exactly characterises mental health, as opposed to the more familiar analyses of ill-health, are also the subject matter of the present book. I have also focused on a number of topical issues, such as male–female relationships and the often neglected question of the role of the father in the family.

Mine is, perhaps not surprisingly, a self-questioning profession. I have not hesitated to look at the way we ourselves operate, and the pros and cons of our own interaction with the family groups with whom we work.

Family Health

*E*arly in my training at the Institute of Psychiatry, that great fountainhead of my profession, I scoured the library thirty years ago for articles and books on what exceptional mental health might mean. I was interested not only in how it differed from the abnormal behaviour I was seeing on the wards, which often wasn't all that different from what one encountered outside, but also from the ordinary, average, batty behaviour I observed in myself and my colleagues, or that one can hear every day (and indeed can now also see) in the House of Commons. It is obvious that some of us function better, others worse, and that we each vary in our state of health from day to day. So, I wondered what was known about the very best functioning possible – what optimal health, health of 'Olympic' standards would be like.

In the end, I found three articles. Two were trivial. But the third was more what I was searching for, an actual attempt to study some people who seemed to function unusually productively and to

1

make good relationships, especially in their marriages. Though the article was impressionistic and carried no weight in a scientific sense – it was based on individuals the author knew personally together with a number of well-known personalities – there was an immediate ring of truth in the findings reported. One observation made a particularly vivid impression. These people appeared to make strong and close relationships with their spouses, yet also seemed not to 'need' them and to function very well independently. One consequence of this was seen when some of them lost their partners through bereavement: they grieved deeply but surprised others by recovering fully and easily to make a new intimate relationship. I can still recall the chill this information struck into me as I read it – did it mean that my warm 'romantic' view of love was unreal, unhealthy? At the same time I found it a strangely liberating idea and had a deep intuitive sense of its truth.

During the next twenty years not much appeared in the research literature to illuminate this neglected field. But in my clinical work with individuals, groups, families and couples the question of what constitutes mental health continued to be a central interest. And in 1976 my first text book of marital and family therapy recorded what I had learned about the nature of health, and expressed one crucial finding, echoing that first paper I

2

encountered, in its title: *One Flesh: Separate Persons*.

By curious coincidence, my book's American editor, who brought me my first copy on a business visit to London, presented me at the same time with another book her company had published in the same month. This was *No Single Thread*, the first research study into a number of exceptionally healthy families. For some weeks it disrupted my life as, unable to put it down, I let my tea go cold, over-ran my normal bus stops, kept my patients waiting, neglected my wife and children, and generally allowed my mental ill-health to show even more than usual.

During this time a letter arrived from an American colleague, whose name and institution were then unknown to me. It said how interested he was in the similarities between my conclusions about health, based on clinical findings, and some research results that he and his team had turned up. I was still too absorbed in the new book to give this letter more than cursory attention, and it was some time before I noticed its senior author had the same name as my correspondent. I then realised we were reading each other's books, both of us excited by the support each gave, from quite different types of study, to the findings of the other.

The following year, 1977, George Vaillant's *Adaptation To Life* reported the findings of a psychological study of mental health among an

3

outstanding group of graduates of Harvard University, whose members had been followed-up over a period of forty years. A bit earlier, in 1970, Westley and Epstein's *Silent Majority* had looked at the families of university students to see what features correlated with particular academic success and other effective functioning. There have been a few other contributions since, but there still isn't much.

Nevertheless, even as it stands our little stock of knowledge about very high levels of mental health must be among the most valuable information our human race possesses. Despite its small volume, the general principles which emerge from the existing findings are very clear and there is a striking lack of any significant disagreement among them. Moreover, this agreement is true not only of the research on exceptional mental health, but also when one includes the more usual comparisons of mental disorder with 'normal' behaviour in the sense of average, mid-range functioning – that is, the way most of us operate – provided that one makes allowance for differences in concepts and in the range of levels of health being measured.

It is indeed the only yardstick we have by which to judge everything else in our family, social and community relationships, and to guide our political policies intelligently, apart from blind adherence to a doctrine of one kind or another. And since the findings about optimal health happen to echo many fundamental tenets of the most influential ethical and religious teachings, they could help us towards the set of shared values we need, in this age of integration, which could command respect both from the religious and from those who require rules to be underpinned by fact and rational argument.

Yet the most interesting thing about our knowledge of mental health is the almost total lack of interest shown in the information since it has become available. This is particularly the case in the mental health professions, who might have been expected to leap upon it exultantly. Why is this potential treasure being ignored? I have come to realise that people at each different level of mental health have different ideas about what being healthy means. Each level therefore sees itself as 'normal' and sees other levels, those above as well as those below, as less healthy. Hence my discomfort on learning about the spouses, described in that first article I found, who recovered readily from the death of their loved ones and so threatened my need at that time for a clinging attachment.

I was lucky then to be in a receptive frame of mind, and that painful information about the need for separateness as well as commitment, which later came to me from all directions in my clinical work and was eventually confirmed by the research mentioned above, sustained me and completely   5 transformed the anguish of my own bereavement in 1987. I think this information about optimal health could therefore help us all to move a notch or two up the scale, even if we never win the mental health Olympics, and a starting point must be this fundamental need for space as well as togetherness.

Big Baby on Board

Which is best to aim for in relationships, space or togetherness? The question is faulted, for we cannot have one without the other. Too much space starves us, too much togetherness suffocates. All relationships involve distance after we emerge from our mother's womb, and require a balance between these two extremes.

Research on healthy families, and clinical experience, indicates that the ability to find a balance between these two poles is particularly vital to emotional health. Unhealthy families find it difficult to attain it at all. Mid-range, 'average', families achieve it in a rigid way which impairs the quality of the relationship. But exceptionally healthy families seem able to have the best of both worlds. The 'optimally' healthy families studied by the Timber-lawn Research Foundation in Dallas, Texas (yes, Dallas!), headed by Dr Jerry M Lewis, showed an ability to move easily back and forth between emotional intimacy and enjoyable independent functioning, together with a pattern of long-term marital fidelity. There was also considerable sharing of parental roles, despite clear differences between them, and both partners collaborated in managing closeness and distance.

Families at the lower end of the health-scale are tightly enmeshed with one another and find it hard to operate independently, especially when in close proximity to one another. There is no name for this whole group of families where members tend to 'live in each other's pockets', and in our book *Families and How to Survive Them* John Cleese and I had to invent one. We called them 'fuzzy families'.

The more severe forms of mental illness – like schizophrenia and manic-depressive disorder – show this enmeshed family pattern in more extreme form. But the remainder of these 'fuzzy families' cope with life adequately unless exposed to powerful stresses, and find ways to protect themselves against the fear of being engulfed and losing what individuality they possess.

This group includes the multi-problem families which are often a nightmare to the social services, but many rich and powerful families also fit the description and their advantages can provide interesting ways of coping. One such family had solved the problem by operating a chain of department stores in different American cities. They could remain closely involved through the business, but were able to live five hundred miles apart, each supervising a store. Some families need whole oceans between them, with each member living in a different continent.

In a couple who attended sessions for marital difficulties the wife joined a therapy group and gradually became more differentiated, but after the interview her businessman husband literally took flight and spent much of the next few years airborne, visiting other countries, before her clearer boundaries began to define his own in turn.

'Mid-range' families – that majority of us who form the sixty per cent or more in the middle of the health scale – are less intensely involved and so do not need these extreme solutions, but show difficulties over distance-regulation of lesser degree. The traditional, role-segregated marriage, where differences between men and women are emphasised and the even greater psychological similarities avoided, so that each occupies a different 'territory' as in an Irish dance hall, is the most universal solution at this level. He gives his main attention and time to his job, while she gives hers to the children.

Within this role division, responsibility for ensuring closeness is usually taken on by the female, that for distance by the male. To use a nautical analogy, she is in charge of the grappling irons and tries to make him stay home more, while he is in charge of the fenders, complains about her possessiveness

9

and finds excuses to be out doing other things. This arrangement maintains a distance that is in fact necessary to them both, as they soon discover if they come into therapy and one of them begins to change.

What happens then resembles those cartoons where an ardent male chases a female across the screen, only to reappear running in the opposite direction because she now wants to surrender and is chasing him. One consequence of the emancipation and empowerment of women has been a reversal of this kind, where the female is increasingly involved in interests outside the home and it is the man who wants more cosy domesticity. Either way, this divided responsibility puts them in opposition and can be a source of endless conflict.

When fears of closeness mount, as often happens as a marriage progresses, affairs are a frequent solution. Many motives contribute to infidelity, but fear of fusion, and a need to bring in a third party to lessen the threat of complete loss of independence, is the most common factor. It is astonishing to what extent psychological dynamics are akin to the laws of physics, and where an affair is taking place I find it helps couples if I compare their situation to that of a spacecraft between the earth and the moon.

At the point where the gravitational attraction of the earth and moon are balanced, the spacecraft is in a sense 'free' and not in the power of either. But if it moves too far in either direction from this point of balance, it suffers an increasing gravitational pull and, unless it can resist this attraction, it is captured and crashes. While infidelity must always be painful for the injured party, understanding of these dynamics at least helps this spouse to see that the infidelity is not basically due to failure on their part and so at least makes it less wounding in a personal sense. Indeed, the affair is often a reaction to too great an attachment, though of a dependent, child–parent kind, rather than a loss of involvement.

This explains reactions which do not seem to fit with our 'common-sense' expectations. A husband who was compulsively unfaithful throughout his marriage ceased his affairs and began to seek the intimacy and tenderness his wife had always asked for as soon as she became less clinging and even gave him permission to have other women. Once she threw the 'grappling irons' overboard, he could safely come alongside without fear of being boarded and taken over. However, she now became temporarily disturbed as she had to face her own fears of closeness, which she had never had to encounter while he was maintaining the distance for them both.

All these problems stem from childhood needs we have not outgrown. A good marriage can give us a second chance to fulfil and move beyond these needs, provided the process is two-way, and as 11 long as their real nature is not hidden in the disguise of reasonable adult expectations for 'loyalty', 'love', 'togetherness', 'freedom', etc. Until this happens, perhaps we should wear stickers like those one sees in car rear windows: 'Keep Your Distance – Big Baby On Board'!

How can we find a better balance? Even seeing more clearly what is causing the problems, and the direction in which we need to go to find something better, starts the process off.

Too Much of a Good Thing

Why has the growing research on exceptionally healthy families been so strangely neglected? One reason, I believe, is that the knowledge can be discouraging unless we pay attention to how those born less fortunate can benefit from it. Envy can be a powerful force towards beneficial change if the gulf between us and the envied state appears bridgeable, when we call it 'admiration'. If not, envy becomes destructive and seeks a solution by denying or destroying what is admired.

In describing the various factors that combine to produce optimally healthy families, it is therefore worth pausing each time to see how we can all benefit from what they tell us.

In couples I see professionally, the problems of the overwhelming majority are due to levels of attachment – need for nurture and support – which are very high and focused too exclusively on the partner. As a result, the relationship suffers overload and one or both partners feels trapped, enslaved, unable to escape from a role of childish dependence. With some couples this is overt and obvious enough to outsiders. In others the dependency is countered by distance-maintaining mechanisms which incur high costs in energy and diminished quality of life, but merely hide the excessive attachment without modifying it. Physical distance; separate territories or roles for each partner; passivity, silence, sulking and other forms of emotional withdrawal; or open conflict more to create a 'no-man's-land' buffer zone than to find a solution.

What are the roots of this over-attachment? From the time we emerge from our mother's body and the umbilical cord is cut, the process of becoming a separate individual continues (or should continue) throughout life. The sustenance originally drawn from her very blood, then her milk, is gradually replaced by an increasing variety of foods, supplied and prepared by a wider range of people.

For emotional health, the same should happen as regards emotional support. Ideally the father shares in caring for the infant from an early stage (the importance of this sharing by the father in the nurturing function is a regular finding in the research on healthy families). And then grandparents, uncles and aunts, brothers and sisters, playmates from neighbouring homes or playgroups, and school friends all add to an ever-widening network of attachment.

Provided the mother has felt secure by receiving adequate support herself, and enjoyed her maternal function, she will have laid a good foundation of confidence in the child's early stages. And if she can also bear to share her once-exclusive possession with these other carers, the child's emotional security becomes nourished by a great root-system of support which can survive separation from, or even the loss of, large parts of it.

Jealousy plays an important and positive part in this process. The very idea of being separate, different, autonomous, cannot arise until one has experience of three-person relationships. One then *sees* two separate individuals in a changing relationship, closer emotionally at one time and more distant at another, while at the same time one *experiences* being sometimes included in that relationship, sometimes excluded and alone. Thus the parental sexual relationship, and the child's vague awareness that there is something very enjoyable and exciting going on between them from which it is excluded, heightens the child's awareness of being a separate individual. It also strongly motivates the child to grow up and leave home in due course, so that it can find its own mate and enjoy similar fulfilment outside the family.

As with loss and separation, jealousy is often viewed as if it were an exclusively negative force. Now that knights no longer don armour and engage in jousting contests to win their fair ladies – jealousy as a lively spectator sport – its potential for facilitating confidence and autonomy and generating pleasurable excitement is ignored. Yet I would be glad to have as many hot dinners as I have seen couples where discovery of a brief infidelity has fanned the dying embers of their sexual relationship, or brought it to life for the first time. What happened was that they began to look at and appreciate each other as real people again, after coming to take each other so much for granted that they no longer even saw each other, let alone took an interest in what was there to be seen.

What's the bottom line? One of the most positive aspects of working with couples and families is seeing how early failures in the family of origin can be made good in the experience of marriage and bringing up children. The aphorism, 'It's never too late to have a happy childhood', is correct.

But much of the guidance we receive from society, whether from the pulpit or from popular songs, is wrong. Being 'all in all to each other' too often ends in being all too much for each other in a state of stifling boredom.

To avoid overloading the relationship and making impossible demands on one another, each partner needs to preserve some measure of separate as well as shared life, enjoying evenings out with the boys – or girls – and continuing at least some of their past interests and friendships. They will each be more alive, more interesting to each other, have more to talk about and to share.

This mutual permission to continue to grow and change also means that there constantly *is* something new to see and appreciate.

However, the changes will rarely be synchronised. Growth in the two members of a couple is like leap-frog. One suddenly develops new confidence, capacities and interests. The other experiences this as a loss, as rejection by the partner, or as painful inadequacy. All being well, this is felt as a challenge and stimulates a new phase of growth in the one left behind, and after a period of struggle they leap-frog and are ahead again.

As this occurs there will inevitably be periods of conflict. Avoidance of natural argument and struggle is a major cause of stuck and deadened relationships, and a major task of a marital therapist is to open up and referee conflicts that have been avoided and never resolved.

Can one achieve this without a referee? There are a few simple rules and here again the laws governing the physical, psychological and spiritual realms are similar. Most criticism contains truth, and contrary to popular lore we are more likely to express the truth, or the more painful truths, in moments of temper, albeit with much untruth and exaggeration added. Separating out that truth from   17 the rest is like digesting food. Having fully fought our corner and put our case, we need to swallow the criticism – by neither rejecting it nor capitulating, but just living with it for twenty-four hours before replying again. An automatic process of digestion will then take place, provided we do not interfere with it by continuing the argument internally. As with food, the rubbish will be eliminated and the truth will be extracted to nourish us and make us, and the relationship, stronger.

Discovering Dad

*A*t the time I began working in child guidance clinics in the late 1950s fathers had yet to be discovered. It was then the custom to work mainly with the referred child and with the mother in separate interviews. From what little knowledge we had, fathers were understood to be a wild, unpredictable species, given to violent rages if they were not fed on the dot, and uncontrolled, animal-like behaviour at night that disturbed the smooth running of the household and created extra laundry.

Occasional sightings of these fearsome creatures would be reported, usually when they were sitting outside the clinic in cars waiting to pick up their spouse and child after their sessions were over. In these habitats they appeared deceptively unthreatening, but we knew very well that fathers were generally unreliable, or harsh, or unfair, or more trouble than the children themselves, or never at home, and so better kept well away from the real tasks of child-rearing except under the strictest supervision. We had this information about their 19 real nature on the best authority, from the mothers themselves, and who should know better than those living with them in the field?

Admittedly, when we pressed for details the evidence was often sparse. We would learn no more than that they left their socks lying about or put up rickety shelves. But our familiarity with depth psychology made it easy for us to understand that these little aberrations were just a hint of the nameless horrors lurking underneath.

I think it was in 1958 that fathers were officially recognised. In that year I found two articles in child psychiatry journals describing experiences of involving fathers in the treatment of children's problems, with very positive results and no reported injuries. But even before this, from the early 1950s, extraordinary reports had been appearing in the American professional literature about experiments of working with whole families, as a new way of helping when one member presented with an emotional problem of some kind.

In 1962, when my colleagues and I began using this method at the clinics and children's hospitals where I worked, we were surprised to find that most fathers not only came willingly to the sessions, but were puzzled that we had not asked them before.

More often than not it would be the other children, not perceived as problems (at least at that moment), who would show what intervention was needed. In the case of behaviour problems which had not responded to treatment of the child and mother alone, the other children would usually say that the father allowed them all to get away with too much and should be more strict. They would often add that the mother was too kind and easy with them, and that she was inconsistent in both demanding the father's intervention and support over discipline, while criticising him for being heavy-handed and thereby sabotaging his efforts when he complied.

In large numbers of cases where we had formerly invested many months or years of time and effort with slow or limited results, we found families returning after a few such family interviews, or often even one, with shining happy faces and reports that not only had the present problem disappeared, but that the whole family was getting on better. Similar experiences were reported by family therapists all over the world, and the importance of the father's involvement, especially in matters of control but also in nurture, was confirmed by research comparing families suffering emotional problems with those not so afflicted.

In the most severe mental disturbance one parent was found to be carrying the whole burden of responsibility while the other was crushed and ineffectual or peripheral and opting out. Usually the

21

central figure would be a mother who was unable to maintain any consistent structure, while the father had abandoned any attempt to play a part in guiding family affairs; but the reverse of this pattern also occurred. Looking at all these studies (for those interested, I have summarised some of the findings in *One Flesh: Separate Persons* and *Explorations with Families*) one saw the same pattern over and over again: as one moved from looking at the structure of families producing more disturbed children, to those producing less disturbed or well-adjusted children, the father became more central, taking more responsibility and becoming a more respected figure.

Since about the end of the Second World War, the role of the father had been increasingly devalued. And at the time when family therapy was developing in Britain on a big scale – the late 1960s and early 70s – the student revolution and women's movement were at their peak. Authority generally, and the limit-setting function of the father in particular, were under maximum attack. The findings of family therapy provided a valuable counterweight to the extremes of this social swing, showing the harm to which inadequate structure and authority could lead in family life. However, as family therapy replaced the previous mother/child-centred methods of treatment, the new respect for the role of the father was accompanied, in the early years at least, by a corresponding devaluation of that of the mother. Fathers were encouraged to be more forceful, to challenge the mothers who were increasingly viewed as over-involved, over-possessive and encouraging infantilism.

The new methods worked marvellously, but I at least felt that something vital had been lost in changing over to them. Also, I was aware that I was living a contradiction, for though it was most effective to help the father play a more central part in the more disturbed, chaotic families, in other cases I would experience the need to reduce the father's power and work towards a more democratic structure.

What we still lacked was information about really healthy families. In 1976 this arrived with the publication of *No Single Thread*, the book which reported on the work of J Lewis and his colleagues at the Timberlawn Research Foundation in Dallas, Texas. Now everything fell into place. The sickest families, they found, were chaotic and lacking in structure. The mothers were central but ineffective and unable to exercise control, while fathers had opted-out or were excluded. Mid-range, more 'average' families provided structure and safe control, but usually through a rigid hierarchy and values which were not open to question. Most often the structure was based on the traditional gender stereotypes, with the father dominant. Most of our clinical work had involved moving families from the first (chaotic) towards this second (mid-range) category.

The good news was that in the most healthy families of all the structure was clear but flexible. The parents were prepared to provide firm government when necessary, but where possible they reached decisions by discussion and negotiation with the children. Most pleasing of all was the observation that the fathers and mothers in these 'optimal' families were able to collaborate and share power equally.

What Are Fathers For?

Working with whole families made us more aware of the importance of the father's role. It was not that we learned that fathers were more important than mothers in child development, but that they had a vital part to play in the family team which had been neglected in recent times.

What is this essential contribution the father needs to make? Research indicates that in the most healthy families the father and mother share power and are able to work together harmoniously at the child-rearing task. It also seems to work best if they play basically different roles, but with considerable overlap in some areas, especially in providing nurture and support. But exactly what those differences in role should be are not made very clear in the conclusions.

When families in treatment are asked in the course of family interviews what role they need the father to play in order to function more happily, both the children and the mothers tend to give very consistent answers in line with the traditional role of the father – particularly over control and limit-setting – and to improve when he begins to fulfil this.

The main problem I have met in this aspect of family work has been in getting the father to accept a greater level of responsibility and the corresponding authority needed to fulfil it. Why is this so? All taking of authority is a lonely business, incurring temporary unpopularity, so that one needs to be sufficiently independent to stand alone at times. And while men are taught to conceal their dependence on others, that training in fact tends to make them less strong than their womenfolk, who can more easily admit weakness and overcome it by seeking support from their partner and from other women. The conventions of family life and male/female relationships cover up this male vulnerability efficiently, but it is very clearly seen in the course of the treatment of couples in groups. The traditional 'me Tarzan, you Jane' arrangement, where the husband is covertly supported on his unsteady pedestal by a vaguely complaining wife, has usually broken down as the wife's self-awareness and consequent dissatisfaction have grown.

Once in therapy, the woman's dissatisfaction becomes more openly expressed. The man is bewildered, since he never noticed there was anything wrong before and doesn't think he has changed at all. He hasn't, and this is the trouble; because she *has* changed, and wants to change more, and fears this would lead to the end of the relationship unless he changes too. He will say he has always been satisfied with the marriage (as well he might be; up to this point she has agreed to a very uneven deal) and is satisfied with her even now. This failure to criticise her which I think she sees, correctly, as a failure even to see her as a person, seems to infuriate women most of all. If you ask him what he wants at this point, he can rarely give a clear answer, for as long as she is automatically anticipating and adapting to his needs he will have no reason to be aware of them. He can be relied upon to say he only wants a quiet life, which is the one thing he's not going to get from now on – until, that is, he ultimately begins to wake up and fight his corner. What never ceases to amaze me, at this point, is the force of the conditioning which inhibits the woman from criticising the man straight-forwardly, and obliges her to continue to prop him up.

Later it becomes clearer why the woman doesn't 'go for the jugular'. He is in her power as long as she shields him from the truth about himself, and he will sense this uneasily, feeling all the more anxious because the gravity and extent of the weaknesses she is holding over him – or protecting him from, whichever way you like to look at it – are never made clear. With encouragement, the woman eventually stops pulling her punches and 'lets him have it'. The man first reels under the impact but in the end has no alternative but to fight back, because it is now clear that she can no longer be manipulated instead through guilt (over being a nag, a 'castrating woman' etc.). The worm finally turns, battle is joined, and the bird, instead of getting the worm, now begins to get some of her own medicine.

The struggle that follows varies in duration and intensity. It may be resolved quickly, or it may involve periods of fierce antagonism or temporary separations. It ends when one or other of the partners is really able to stand on his or her own feet. When this happens the other partner will also have to change and learn to do the same, or will leave or be left.

If they both continue to 'hang in there', as they usually do when supported through this difficult stage, a relationship ensues where both are more independent (and in consequence more interesting to each other), but at the same time able to be closer and more intimate and to share more of their lives. As seen by others, they are often happy to continue in a relationship that superficially may appear quite traditional, or they may follow some other style; such details do not seem very important. But the relationship is completely changed. They are now, in the words I used for the title of my first book: 'one

28

flesh: separate persons', closer to the combination of loving intimacy, and of self-sufficiency and independence, that is so striking in optimally healthy families. Once this is possible, the relationship is no longer a necessity anxiously clung to, but a luxury, a bonus which can just be enjoyed and held lightly, where the partners give both pleasure and freedom to each other.

The way this process appears to onlookers, however, is that the man has to become a match for the woman; even, to start with, just a little bit more than a match for her if she is to feel safe to be truly herself without destroying his self-esteem as a man. Outwardly this looks so close to the traditional pattern of 'male domination' that – doubting myself in typical male fashion – I asked my late wife (who shared the couples'-group work with me until her death) why the women we saw always wanted the man to draw the line and make clear what he would and would not put up with from her. 'Because it sets the woman free,' she answered. 'Once he does that, the woman can use her full strength without worrying about what it will do to him. Then she can come into her own.' And so, happily, can he, as a man, a husband and a father.

More on Fatherhood

*H*ow do we read the feelings of others? My studies in trying to relate emotions to posture and facial expression convinced me that we do so by imitating other people's bodily expressions, because this automatically produces an echo in us of what they are feeling. In other words, in order to put ourselves in the position of someone else emotionally, copying their 'position' is literally how we achieve it.

The movements involved in this mimicry are so restrained and slight that we are unaware it is happening at all; and of course, if our mimicry was more pronounced it could be misunderstood and offensive to others. Once alerted to this fact, one can observe the process happening and develop greater emotional sensitivity. This automatic resonance to one another's feelings prompts us to respond in ways that will meet each other's needs. The distress of a child will normally evoke in adults an impulse towards close attention and care, though this biological safety mechanism can fail disastrously, as it did with so many onlookers in the Bulger case.

At other times, children's fears of losing control of themselves and causing harm to their parents or damaging their relationship with them evokes a response of firmness and limit-setting in the latter. What the adults are responding to when they do this is usually described as 'naughtiness'. The children show their need for firmer control by increasing their own loss of self-control, and parents usually experience a reaction of anxiety and then anger, which triggers the actions that once again bring the situation under control. The children's anxiety over their destructive impulses then reduces and they regain control of themselves so that, no longer needing to provoke the parents' anger because it has already appeared and done its necessary work, the 'naughtiness' subsides.

But if the parents' reaction is too bland or reasonable, the children will automatically increase their provocation until the parents are pushed beyond their tolerance to a point where, finally, they firmly take charge to stop the misbehaviour. This imposition of order in response to increasing chaos can – and does – come from either parent, but traditionally it has been regarded as the particular responsibility of the father.

When I began experimenting with interviews with whole families, I was quickly struck by the passivity of fathers in those families where children were referred for behaviour disorders. They frequently seemed to leave responsibility for discipline to the mother and let her suffer the subsequent unpopularity while they remained 'Mr Nice Guy'.

And I repeatedly found that, if the father could be activated to take more responsibility for limit-setting, the behaviour problems quickly diminished. This connection was more true of children with phobias and obsessional disorders and improvement was usually even more rapid. These dynamics also develop between therapists and patients, who readily fall into child and parent roles with one another. Interactions of this kind are often the richest source of information the therapist gets about the cause of the family problems, and can provide not only a clear reflection of the underlying family relations but also an opportunity to change them.

In more normal families, children probably know well that if they don't do what they are told they will get a good smack and/or be sent to bed with no supper, so they stop their nonsense.

This principle that every social system, from a family to a nation, needs at least one person taking on the responsibility to prevent it behaving in too self-destructive a way, has often presented itself to me in all kinds of group situations – small and large.

When working with the staff group at a day
32 hospital, it became clear that in times of anxiety and

stress the consultant had to take a clearer, commanding role. Even if he didn't actually 'take the wheel', he at least appeared to be staying 'on the bridge', ready to give orders or answer queries. In other words, to be 'reassuringly in charge'.

In one factory I visited there were complaints that the managing director was too authoritarian. In fact, he was too keen to be liked and too permissive, and the company ran more smoothly when he distanced himself from his staff and took on a clearer role.

In *Three Corvettes*, an account of his experience of the role of authority in group relations in vessels on active service, author Nicholas Monsarrat looked at these issues from the viewpoint of a midshipman, a second-in-command and a commander. A good captain is someone who is a 'decent old bastard', respected because he is firm but fair. If he is too soft, too keen to be liked, the ship isn't painted and rusts, and the gunners don't learn to shoot straight and hit targets.

You will note that I refer to 'he'. Why 'he'? Does it have to be the father, or a male? I have already said that both parents can, and do, perform this role – increasingly so as children grow older. But I cannot escape the evidence of my experience that it seems more difficult for the mother if she has, as is more often the case, been the main care-giver early on. And fathers have, or used to have, the advantage of a greater emotional distance.

33

But in later childhood I don't think this applies in the same way. And in larger social systems beyond the family, there is even less argument for it. In industry, for example, there are many female managing directors controlling their systems as effectively as any man.

Margaret Thatcher was regarded by the Conservative Party, and much of the country, as the best man that Parliament could field for the job. She also managed to quash an industrial anarchy threatening everyone's future that preceding male Prime Ministers had failed to confront.

So, if a woman can handle a challenge like the battle of Orgreave Colliery as well as, or better than, any man, what are the implications for who can best handle law and order in the family?

I would love to have the answer. But we also need to know to what extent her eventual failure and rejection were a consequence of her inability to bring to her leadership those qualities formerly best exemplified by women in traditional maternal roles. Qualities like the ability to listen and take account of others' views and feelings, to value discussion and agreement, consensus, fairness and the happiness of the whole family, not just part of it.

Talk Amongst Yourselves

*I*n their study of exceptionally healthy families, Dr Jerry Lewis and his colleagues at the Timberlawn Research Foundation, Dallas, Texas, found very clear and striking differences in some of the ways they functioned when compared both with families producing sick members, and with the mid-range or 'average' families that make up the middle of the spectrum. I have already mentioned two of these features. First, they have a striking capacity to function well independently, despite their equal ability to sustain close and committed relationships. And second, the parents share power and they easily maintain whatever authority structure is necessary for the family to function efficiently, while reaching decisions wherever possible by consultation and agreement.

A third difference these researchers found among families at different levels of health was in the way they communicated. How families talk among themselves has been a subject of great interest since the beginnings of family therapy in the 1950s, and many of the findings have become well-known and entered the language. The notion of the 'double-bind', an idea developed in American studies of how severely disturbed families talked to one another, was popularised through the books of R D Laing and his colleagues. For those unfamiliar with what it means, the American researchers reported that communication in severely disturbed families often contained two incompatible messages, such that the member spoken to was tied in a knot, could never get it right. In such families, you are 'damned if you do and damned if you don't'. In families, sometimes one message is carried by the words, the other by the tone of voice or some other non-verbal expression. A domineering father may say to a son: 'Why are you so timid, why don't you stick up for yourself?'; or a mother may say: 'Why aren't you more affectionate; why do you never kiss your mummy?', while at the same time making it clear by their expression and attitude that these emotions are the last thing they will tolerate when directed at themselves. There are many other related forms of communication that disqualify or subject the hearer to a put-down. A nice example is the story about the difficult mother who gave her son a present of two ties. When he put one on to show he liked them she asked 'Oh, didn't you like the other one?' In Heller's novel, *Catch-22*, pilots were subjected to the double-bind that if they tried to avoid flying by claiming to have been driven mad by the conditions of their war-service, their reaction was judged sensible and normal, so they must be sane and fit to fly.

Communication in very disturbed families is generally obscure, ambiguous, confusing. Statements do not seem to connect with one another; it is hard for an outsider to get the point or follow the thread. No one will commit themselves. It is impossible to make a clear and honest contract, or to discover any clear and consistent rules that, if followed, would keep one out of trouble. Everyone seems to be covering their own back, seeking advantage or at least fearing and trying to avoid being taken advantage of. The similarity to living in a totalitarian state controlled by someone functioning at this level – Hitler's Germany, Stalin's Russia or Ceaucescu's Romania – is obvious enough.

Turning to the other end of the spectrum of health, the communication in exceptionally healthy families is clear, open and direct. This honesty seems to be possible because of a general feeling of confidence and trust, an assurance that everyone will be listened to respectfully, and accepted and loved for themselves even when there is disagreement or temporary disapproval over some action. The book reporting the Timberlawn findings, *No Single Thread*, describes this nicely: 'Part of the sensation of joy the observer feels in observing the   37 interaction of healthy families is the obvious lack of calculation, the openness of honest feeling and thought on the part of different family members – especially the children. There is freedom without chaos – a feeling of a three-ring circus, yet with everything under control.'

The Timberlawn team in fact found that the family conversation of the most healthy families was *less* clear than that of the mid-range. But the difficulty the observers had in following the family interaction was not due to lack of clarity or the family members failing to understand one another, but rather because they understood each other so well that they could anticipate what was coming next. So statements would be fragmentary, un-finished, and the exchange was often too fast to follow. This contrasted with, in the mid-range or average families, communication which was rigid and constricted, confined within more narrow and rigid limits. The greater clarity of the average families was at the cost of their being more pedantic and controlled.

The description of very healthy families as like a 'three-ring circus, yet with everything under con-trol' dispels an illusion some people hold that healthy families are merely less liable to the power-ful and potentially disturbing emotions that plague the mentally sick, just less *un*healthy rather than possessing additional and different qualities. The natural assumption is that even if they may be more contented, they must be dull and boring. Though there is in fact some truth in this as one moves from the sickest families to the average or mid-range, the reverse is true as one moves from mid-range to maximum health. In this as in many other respects there seems to be a sort of 'gear-change' in moving from average to optimal health, rather than just 'more of the same'. The most healthy seem to achieve control not so much by restriction and repression of strong feeling, as the mid-range tend to do, as by their unusual capacity to balance and manage a wide spectrum of emotions instead of keeping the lid on them. This is no doubt one explanation for the playfulness, humour and creativity that observers so frequently describe.

It is my belief that the conflictual, paradoxical communication that leads to double-binds and other harmful communication in the least healthy is still present in healthier families but more under conscious control and put to deliberate service in humour, irony, lively banter and teasing. Teasing can of course be malicious, but within the context of affection it helps us to become more sturdy and independent, to accept the adversities of life with a better grace and good humour. I learnt this when my son was eight and my daughter six, and they adored spending the day with Hubert Lewis, a jovial farmer neighbour. One day I asked my son   39

why he enjoyed his time there so much. Did Hubert
tell him all about farming? No. Did he play with
him? No. So what did he do? A beatific smile spread
over his face. 'He *teases* me,' he said.

The Balancing Act

C ontinuing this survey of what we know about the functioning of healthy families, I shall expand the enquiry to see whether the principles may have a wider application.

In the new book that John Cleese and I are writing together, provisionally titled *Life and How to Survive It* [subsequently published under that title in 1993], we are trying to explore the meaning of health on different levels: first on the level of the family; second on the level of organisations, including industry where we seek reasons for the ascendancy of Japanese manufacturing and the relative decline first of our own and more recently of the American industrial scene, where each country earlier led the world. Thirdly, we then try to see if one can speak meaningfully of more healthy and less healthy societies, and if so – here we move to a fourth level – what value systems seem to enable societies to function at their best.

Our first book, *Families and How to Survive Them*, was not only well-received by the public but despite its unusual form was also, to my surprise and relief, sufficiently approved by my profession for the pair of us to be invited to address a variety of professional bodies – the Association of Child Psychology and Psychiatry, the Association of Family Therapy, the National Marriage Guidance Council, the Tavistock Clinic and several others. More recently, the book has also become widely enough known in the United States for the American Family Therapy Association, at their annual conference in Philadelphia two weeks ago, to invite us to speak to them. In doing so we drew upon the broader study of health in our second book, to throw light upon some questions the conference was considering about professional work with families.

The conference was entitled 'Back To The Future In Philadelphia', because one day was given over to a review of the origins of family therapy in the 1950s and a look at where it might be going in the 1990s. As part of this, John and I were asked to say something about how these developments had looked when seen from abroad, at least from our perspective. I focused on the American family and the attitudes and approaches of American family therapists, as seen from another culture, based partly on my professional work with couples and families from the United States temporarily living in England, who for some reason have always formed more than a quarter of my practice. As John had no professional knowledge of family work, he spoke on a wider scale about some of his impressions of American society.

In our work together, we have repeatedly found that whether we are looking at the level of individual and family health, or industrial efficiency and innovation, or societies that facilitate all of these, each level turns out to be operating on the same small number of simple principles when they are functioning at their best. One of these fundamental principles which has turned up over and over again is the requirement for some optimum balance between the value given to the individual on the one hand and the value given to the group on the other; that is, to the part and to the whole.

Many of the problems family therapists have to deal with stem from this imbalance between respect for the individual and respect for the welfare of the community. One consequence is the uncertainty and confusion American families and parents – and countries strongly influenced by the US like Britain – experience nowadays about child-rearing and male/female relationships and responsibilities. The excesses of the 'me' generation, of what Christopher Lasch labelled 'the culture of narcissism' and what in Texas I found they disapprovingly called the process of 'Californication', have inflicted terrible damage in the way they have led to expectations in couples that each should have all 43 their needs gratified all the time, without considering the partner and no longer expecting to undergo the personal effort, struggle and compromise which were taken for granted in the past. When applied to the family, this emphasis on the individual has made parents uncertain about their right and duty to guide and discipline their children in terms of a clear and socially responsible value-system, with a consequent breakdown in social order, steady increases in delinquency and crime, epidemics of drug addiction, and other social ills.

The same point about the unbalanced emphasis on the individual was made by John Cleese quoting book titles like *Eat To Win* and *Zen Gives You The Competitive Edge*, and also remarks by American football, baseball and basketball coaches promoting such extreme competitiveness in sport that winning becomes all important and sportsmanship is increasingly devalued: 'Winning is not everything, it's the only thing'; 'Nice guys finish last'; 'Show me a good loser and I'll show you a player I'm going to trade'; 'Defeat is worse than death, because you have to live with defeat.' As usual, what he had to say was very funny, all the more so because the Four Seasons Hotel in Philadelphia, justly reputed as one of the most efficient and helpful in the country, inevitably developed a touch of the *Fawlty Towers* on the morning before our lunchtime

44

address. John had been revising his speech into a dictaphone the day before, and when he asked the hotel for a secretary to type it out every imaginable thing went wrong. As the minutes ticked inexorably away *Fawlty Towers* turned into *Clockwise* and he arrived at the lecture hall on the dot but still with only the first half of his speech. Mercifully, hotel staff came running through the door in the nick of time, waving the next page in the air as he got to the end of the last in his hand. He is at his best in such crises, so I was enjoying it as much as the audience who probably thought it was all a put-up job. The humour would have made anything palatable and John had rather spiked the audience's guns by his final question asking why Americans were so touchy and fearful of criticism, but we were surprised and impressed to see how warmly our critical remarks were received.

Is there a solution to this imbalance? If the US operates on the basis of individualism, competition and adulation of 'stars', my experience of the Japanese is that two of their most basic ground rules are 'We are all one big happy family' and 'The nail that sticks up gets knocked down.' They have their own social and family problems, stemming from this emphasis on the group at the expense of the individual. But I believe that the imbalances in these two countries, which are now so intimately and uncomfortably bound together, will help to 45

find a better balance for them both and that we in
Britain will profit from this exchange as well.

All You Need Is Love

*O*f the ingredients which make for maximum mental health in individuals and families, there is one which seems most important of all. The Timberlawn Research team in Dallas who tracked down families enjoying emotional health of 'Olympic' standards, found that they showed what the researchers called an 'affiliative attitude' towards others.

'Affiliative' meant that the very healthy families had a positive attitude towards human encounter. Their view of human nature was essentially benign. They typically reached out, showed friendliness and warmth, were caring and helpful in their relationships and had a basic expectation that others would, in the main, be positive and friendly to them as well. This didn't mean that they were unrealistic or easily deceived. They could protect themselves against abuse of such friendliness, but typically they would give others the benefit of the doubt. By contrast, the attitude towards others in both unhealthy and mid-range families tended to be oppositional rather than affiliative. In the sickest

47

families this negative attitude was more extreme, to the point of overt hostility, chronic fear of rejection or betrayal, suspicion to the point of paranoia, bitterness, resentment and other negative emotions which would either make them avoid relationships altogether or spoil them if they developed.

In the mid-range, 'average' families the oppositional attitude took milder forms but still embodied a pessimistic, distrustful view of human nature. Because people were seen to be just out for themselves and likely to take advantage, these families felt it was important not to trust others very far and to concentrate on 'looking after Number One'. It was better to keep to yourself, keep your distance, not give yourself away, keep things as far as possible within the family. And be watchful even there.

What is new here? Nothing. Most of us were told this at our mother's or grandmother's knee, and if we were lucky we learnt it by having the attitude demonstrated in practice towards us. They would just have called it 'love', not affiliative attitude, but that one word now means so many things that a piece of jargon has to be substituted in scientific research so that it is clear which meaning is intended.

One kind of 'love' is exemplified by the boy scout who is reproved by the scoutmaster for not turning up on time:

'You're late!'

'I know, sir; I was helping an old lady across the road.'

'But you're very, *very* late!'

'I know sir; but you see, she didn't want to go.'

Alas, there is all too much of this kind of loving helpfulness in the world, from having the floor vacuumed under one's legs as one tries to read the Sunday papers, to being rescued by Mrs Whitehouse from the danger of watching television programmes that might have been too exciting.

A second meaning is 'do as you would be done by', what one might call an Old Testament kind of neighbourliness based on the notion of fair exchange. You give what you expect to get, no more, no less, and the other side of this one is 'an eye for an eye and a tooth for a tooth'. When we don't think we are getting a fair return, love can turn to hate. This is mid-range morality.

A further meaning, closer to what the Timberlawn researchers intend by 'affiliative attitude', is carried by the New Testament advice 'love thy neighbour as thyself'. This *can* still be taken to mean the same as 'do as you would be done by'. But it also has a more profound meaning, not so much an exhortation to fit in to society as a piece of vital information about human psychology, part of an instruction manual about the way we are made and how we can get on together in the most healthy and

49

happy way. The meaning of this at the psychological level is not that we *should* love our neighbour as we love ourselves, but that as a scientific law, whether we like it or not, we *will* be able to treat others with respect and care, and will wish to do so, exactly to the extent that we have seen into ourselves clearly and discovered that we are at root essentially the same as everyone else. Once we see this, we can no longer feel superior to others, or judge and condemn in the same way as before. We can live and let live, accept superficial differences because we are aware of the basic identity beneath. We can still disapprove of harmful behaviour and struggle against tendencies which are malevolent and destructive, in ourselves and others. But we will do so with compassion, making allowances for other people's limitations and handicaps. And our efforts are more likely to be successful and even well-received because they will be more intelligent, in the sense of being based on a deep understanding of others that comes from a real knowledge of our own psychology.

To the extent that we do not know ourselves, we are at the mercy of our most negative emotions, for we will then be unaware of them except as we project them onto others. We will see our own malevolence in the world outside, as if it has nothing to do with us except that it is threatening us.

And here the same law applies. We sow the wind

and reap the whirlwind, die by the sword because we live by the sword, anticipate rejection, meanness or criticism because we are rejecting, mean or critical ourselves and do not see it.

We can grasp this up to a point, but do not easily see the full implications. We can see that someone who has understood and come to terms with themselves might feel different, might get on better with others, would be nice to have around. What we don't see so readily is the extraordinary fact that we all live in totally different worlds, while inhabiting the same geographical space. The more healthy person lives in a more friendly world, because positive attitudes tend to arouse positive reactions. It is not that the unhealthy person just imagines the world is a more difficult, unfriendly place than the more healthy person finds it to be. The negative expectation arouses corresponding negative feelings and behaviour in others and the world then actually *is* more unfriendly and difficult to deal with, other things being equal.

We all experience this, even if we do not realise it. We are all constantly moving up and down the level-of-health-scale as our moods change. We get out of bed on the wrong side, burn the toast, quarrel with our partners, forget something and have to go back to get it, miss the bus, and on the next bus someone steps on our toes, the conductor is rude . . . and so on. We are actually in a different world   51 to the one we inhabited yesterday, when we woke in good spirits, things went well and everyone was nice to us.

Sex and Loving

*I*n writing about the way healthy families operate I have focused on the warm, positive relationships they appear to enjoy not only with each other, but also with neighbours and the community in general. Though they are realistic and can protect themselves against abuse of their benevolence, they have an unusual capacity to function on the basis of love and trust.

As one might expect and hope, it appears that this extends to the sexual relationship as well. One of the earliest studies of health in families, reported by Westley and Epstein in 1969 in their book *Silent Majority*, showed a clear link between the level of health and happiness in families on the one hand, and both frequency of parental sexual intercourse and increasing enjoyment of it, on the other. Children growing up in these families were reported to 'face life with the expectation of rich rewards to be found in intimate social relationships, with an almost unshakeable trust in people and the blessings of marriage, and with confidence in themselves as people and in their attractiveness as men and women'.

By contrast, the 'traditional' families studied, where there was a sharp and rigid division of gender-roles and little sharing of household tasks by the parents (ie closer to the 'mid-range' pattern), showed both a lower level of health and happiness and a low frequency and poor enjoyment of sex between the parents.

The more recent studies by the Timberlawn researchers in Dallas were able to distil out, from those at the top of the health scale who were all producing healthy children, a sub-group where the mental health was exceptional – what I have earlier called the 'Olympic' families. Here in fact the frequency of intercourse varied greatly among different couples, but in each case both parents showed a very high level of satisfaction and enjoyment of their sexual relationship. It formed an important part of their close bond and no doubt contributed to the pattern of long-term marital fidelity already mentioned.

The next level down the scale – the 'adequate' families which were number two in the mental health olympics and managing to bring up healthy children even if with a lot of struggle and effort – in fact showed higher frequencies of intercourse between the parents than many 'optimals' but with much lower levels of enjoyment at least as far as the wives were concerned. One gains the impression from the reports that the husbands were more easily contented as long as their need for purely physical release was met, while the wives were distressed that physical sex was not an integral part of a deep and shared emotional life.

Clinical work also confirms this connection between satisfying sexual love and mental health. In working with the emotional problems of children the connection with parental unhappiness soon becomes clear, and this has led many professionals to work with the whole family rather than the children alone.

Often quite rapid improvements can be brought about in the whole family situation if any sexual difficulties that emerge are tackled directly. Good sex is such a profound pleasure, and has such a beneficial effect in dissolving painful and angry feelings and promoting feelings of health and well-being, that a small improvement in this aspect of the parental relationship can have effects as profound and far-reaching as a little extra money can bring to a family under severe financial hardship. This improvement is often reported by the children, even though they do not necessarily know, or are even interested in, the cause of the change.

For example, in *One Flesh: Separate Persons* I described one family where the children showed various problems, stemming from the parents'   55 sexual unhappiness over the previous five years. The basic relationship was good, the problem a simple one of ignorance and prudishness in the parents' families of origin. It was only necessary to negotiate a fresh contract and to provide some very definite support, in the form of 'doctor's orders' that they should lose control and enjoy themselves as fully as possible in bed, to improve the situation. At the second interview, the parents reported a new sexual happiness, and it radiated from them. The children reflected this also, and the adolescent daughter said, 'I don't know what has happened, but it's completely different at home. Mum and Dad seem happy together again, and I feel happy too.'

Many families can be moved a notch or two up the scale of health by simple interventions of this kind which help the parents to experience and express their sexual love for one another. In doing so one is working at the core of the marriage and family, the major bond which brought the parents together, brought their children into the world, and can continue to sustain them through personal anguish, difficulties in the relationship and external pressures, too. Fortunately, help with problems of this kind, and even with sexual difficulties of a more complex nature, is now widely available not only from many hospitals and child and family guidance clinics, but also from the former marriage guidance councils now renamed RELATE, which have been training special counsellors for many years in the skills needed.

The details of parental sexual problems are as far as possible discussed at separate sessions in which the children are not included, but in my experience they are always aware of sexual unhappiness at least in a general way and can sometimes help to find a solution when all other methods have failed.

When trying to understand the incessant arguments of one couple, I asked their two sons, thirteen and seven, to help me. They were reluctant to comment until their parents encouraged them, when the younger boy showed a striking delicacy of expression, and that his biology lessons had not been wasted, as he said: 'I think the problem is that Mum criticises Dad for trying to fertilise her ovum, and then he retaliates.'

Coping With Bereavement

I have written about how one of the most striking findings of recent research with healthy families noted the capacity of the exceptionally healthy to cope with change and loss, including even bereavement where despite (or probably partly because of) grieving deeply, the bereaved spouse was able to continue to function well and rebuild their life. At the lowest levels of health associated with frank mental illness, change and loss of all kinds threaten whatever precarious stability has been achieved, and the death of a spouse can be particularly devastating. Between these extremes on the health-scale, including the average, 'normal' or 'mid-range' – that is, the great majority of us – bereavement may not be as destabilising as this but we are also unlikely to come through it and continue enjoying life as the most healthy seem able to do. We are more likely to deny the reality of the loss and wish hopelessly to stop time or turn the clock back. But even the knowledge about what healthy functioning is like can help and it certainly sustained me

58

and completely transformed the anguish of my own bereavement in 1987. Facing the pain of the loss squarely seemed to put one in touch again with all the happiest memories and enjoyment of our past life together, so that the pain and sadness at what had been taken away were mixed with and made bearable by feelings of joy that one had at least been fortunate enough to be given such a good experience.

I think, in fact, that many in the mid-range are not facing and feeling their natural grief fully; the way they continue to complain about their loss may indeed be akin to what I call 'bleating', that is *ineffective* complaint, seeking commiseration by making the listener feel guilty if he or she does not feel miserable too. They do this rather than seek understanding and support in facing and bearing their grief long enough for it to do its necessary work of changing the inner world to fit the changed outer world – redrawing the maps the mind uses to navigate by. And it is this feeling of being manipulated into taking on the patient's misery, rather than helping them to bear it and cope with it, which can provoke irritation and impatience.

For the medical profession it is as if the doctor is asked to plunge into the torrent sweeping the patient away, instead of staying safely on the bank from which a rope can be thrown down to help them climb out. Until one clearly understands this 59 difference, it is in fact hard to help with any kind of depressive condition. But once one does understand it and is able to avoid being manipulated – anticipates and allows for the sharp tug on the rope one throws down which is aimed to overbalance us and pull us down too – remarkable new possibilities open up and the chances of beneficial change are vastly increased. When doctors are asked to help in this kind of situation, therefore, they may help most when they confront their patients' attempt to avoid or escape from the suffering the loss inevitably brings and, urging them to face it, support them in doing so.

The idealisation of the partner, and denial of problems in the marriage while it existed, can be seen as part of this avoidance of reality. But there is another way of viewing it. One basis for the choice of marital partner is the maintenance of self-esteem through using others to see oneself in a positive way. If Jill is basically quite an angry person, but has grown up in a family where anger is condemned, she will be at risk of feeling bad whenever her bad temper is expressed, even in a condition of tiredness or PMT. One solution is to marry Jack, a rough, aggressive fellow who, growing up in a combative family where fierceness of expression was seen as the norm and boys were expected and almost encouraged to be rough, gets angry whenever things don't go his way. Now if Jill is in a bad

60

temper, it will provoke Jack to a worse one, and he will provoke her in return. She can then see herself as a basically good-tempered person 'if only it wasn't for Jack', who 'started it all', 'upset her' and obliged her to fight back in self-defence. If she showed any anger or behaved badly, it was 'not her fault'; she is 'not really like that'. The neighbours hear her recount similar stories of Jack's bad behaviour and her struggles to cope with it and, not seeing the actual sequence of the emotional explosions and how Jill has changed the punctuation to put Jack's bad temper at the beginning of the story and her own at the end, sympathise and so help to keep the process going.

Of course, husbands can also take on the role of the justly aggrieved, innocent party, and in the couples I have seen professionally it has more often been the man asserting that he is essentially an easy-going, kindly, good-natured chap who 'only gets upset because his wife is difficult and nags him so much'.

Whichever partner is taking this 'victim' role, while the spouse is alive they are protected against facing a negative aspect of their own personality because the partner in effect carries it for them and can be blamed for the harmful consequences. But if the partner dies, the chickens come home to roost and the surviving spouse is at risk of a depressing loss of self-esteem when the partner is no longer   61 there to rescue them, by his or her bad behaviour, from seeing the painful truth that they behave badly too, and often start the cycle of conflict while blaming others for the results. After bereavement, therefore, the denial machinery is apt to go into overdrive and negative aspects of the marital relationship, however they were formerly explained and excused, will often be excised from the story of the marriage altogether by idealising both the partner and the relationship. Here, too, skilled and supportive counselling may be needed to enable the bereaved person gradually to face the truth, particularly the problematic ways of behaving which the choice of partner previously enabled them to avoid acknowledging.

Skills of the Parent

*T*he family is the institution that shapes almost every person in our society. Despite this, there is an assumption that the skills and techniques of parenthood come naturally and do not have to be learned. Consequently there is little help, support or guidance for parents now that the extended family with its generations of experience has more or less disappeared. It is taken for granted that family mental health will just 'happen' and it is very difficult for people to learn how to deal best with the stresses and strains of family life before they become problems.

Of course, there is a great deal of knowledge around. Between us all, we parents have a vast store of experience if only it could be shared and digested. And many purposes served in the past by the extended family have been taken over by a multitude of professions and agencies. However, the knowledge held by 'experts' is often less helpful than it might be. Though, as their name implies, the 'helping professions' came into being for the benefit of those they are supposed to help, those who belong to them often become possessive of their knowledge and more interested in the practice of their own skills than in passing on their expertise to their clients.

The medical profession, psychiatry included, is no exception to this tendency and is probably more closed and defensive than most. But early in my training I found a remarkable exception in S H Foulkes, a psychoanalyst who became interested in working with patients together in groups, originally to treat soldiers suffering from war neuroses during the Second World War. He later became a consultant at the Maudsley Hospital in London, the main British training centre for psychiatry, and taught his methods to others.

Foulkes realised that a group of patients had, between them, enormous resources of knowledge about the causes of their problems even though each person might be blind to his or her own. So he made it his task to help the group to help itself, through each person coming to realise, understand and trust their own experience. He called this process 'group-analysis', though in ordinary language what happens is best described as 'learning together by sharing experience'. This method of helping people to develop their own skills and confidence has been widely applied to develop the skills of professionals outside psychiatry itself, like

64

GPs, community nurses and teachers. But, until recently, there was still a need for this principle to be applied to parenting: 'helping parents to help themselves'.

Then nine years ago, a child psychotherapist and organisational consultant, Ruth Schmidt Neven, and a family therapist, Carolyn Douglas, became co-directors of a new charity called 'Exploring Parenthood' with the direct aim of providing help and support for all parents. Unlike most organisations then existing, this was based on the idea of partnership between parents and professionals, on health rather than pathology, on prevention rather than cure, on competence rather than failure. Parents would have direct access to it, when they wished to come, rather than through professionals when some serious problem had provided an admission ticket.

This is not to say that parenthood can be taught and learned in any conventional way. The philosophy of Exploring Parenthood is that there is no right way to be a parent, but that there are ways to be a good-enough parent that are right for each family. The organisation has spent a great deal of time working out how to combine the skills of the professional with the understanding and practical experience of parents. And because much of the work with parents is done in groups, parents are encouraged to become a 'community of parents'   65 enabling them to help and support each other without the need for professional involvement. Training is offered to parents so that they can run their own independent parent support groups and encourage the wider dissemination of the information and expertise which Exploring Parenthood has to offer.

The charity's activities are based around a professional team from a wide range of disciplines who are available outside the normal clinic setting, in the evenings and at weekends, to work with parents in a partnership to achieve solutions to problems before they become major difficulties. Good organisation of the workshops ensures that discussions do not turn into 'therapy' but are maintained at a regulated safe depth where real sharing is possible while the independence and privacy of participants is respected. And my experience of attending its general meetings is of a most enjoyable and relaxed 'family atmosphere', a sense of general warmth and care which is hard to describe in words though it may be the most important 'message' the organisation conveys, like a kind of 'model' of healthy family relationships.

An underlying principle of Exploring Parenthood's work is that most if not all social problems that affect families are preventable, a view which I fully share. Prevention is both better and cheaper than cure, but few other organisations are trying to
66

involve themselves with families before the bad things happen. Sadly, most governments behave like householders who skimp on maintenance until the house begins to fall down, or like car-owners who neglect routine servicing until expensive but avoidable breakdowns occur. The resources made available by the state are almost exclusively devoted to coping with the effects of family breakdown including child protection, adoption, fostering and counselling as well as divorce, separation and lone parenting. This is all the more grievous because the structure of Exploring Parenthood makes it extra-ordinarily cost-effective. When compared with conventional services, every pound spent is multi-plied many times in its effects. The professional component is used to help families help them-selves, and to help each other, so that paid professional help becomes less and less necessary as a shared culture of knowledge and mutual support develops among the families.

While Carolyn Douglas continues to guide the development of Exploring Parenthood in Britain, Ruth Schmidt Neven recently moved to Australia and is developing related work there. Her book, *The New Explorers*, is a fascinating account of the experience of setting up the organisation in Britain, together with the principles that emerged about helping families to become more healthy and happy, and the lessons learned about the best way for an organisation of this kind to operate. It is in some ways more helpful than most child-care manuals since it draws on such a large pool of widely different family experiences, and itself gives a sense of the sharing and mutual support that Exploring Parenthood was set up to bring about.

When Not to Play a Straight Bat

*I*n a recent issue of the *Journal of Marital and Family Therapy*, John Gottman, Professor of Psychology at the University of Washington, reports on some fascinating new findings about the causes of marriage breakdown and divorce. Interesting in itself is his claim that though fifty per cent of marriages are now likely to end in divorce in the United States, almost all research had previously been concentrated on its effects and almost none on exactly why and how marriages reach this sad end. What research there was proved almost useless for predicting which couples would part.

He and his team have therefore been exploring how marriages change over time, and trying to find, first of all, what kinds of interaction lead to deterioration or improvement in the relationship. To this end they built a laboratory where they could make videotape recordings of couples interacting, and measured heart rates, the amount of overall restlessness and movement, and other physical signs of emotional arousal, while couples were asked to discuss some major area of disagreement.

In their first study, the experimenters were surprised to find that couples whose hearts beat faster, who sweated more and moved a lot while they were interacting – or even while they were quiet but expecting conflict to break out – all showed deterioration in their relationships over the three years they were studied. The accuracy with which these simple physical measures predicted the future outcome was indeed astonishing. Improvement or deterioration in satisfaction with the marriage could be accurately forecast in ninety-five per cent of the cases they studied, and even the rate at which the relationship would change could be judged from the size of the physical measurements.

Excited by this discovery, they next analysed videotapes to find out what kind of interactions brought about downhill change in those marriages which got worse. They found that conflict itself was not necessarily harmful. Indeed, some patterns of conflict appeared to be beneficial to the relationships even when couples felt upset at the time. And marriages even tended to deteriorate when wives always stayed agreeable and compliant. The main source they found for the dissatisfaction was a pattern they called 'stonewalling'. This is where the husband responds to what his wife is saying by avoiding looking at her, keeping a stiff, distant expression on his face, and failing to give the little nods and other signs by which we indicate that we are taking in what is being said to us.

However, being able to predict dissatisfaction in this way still didn't enable divorce to be predicted, since many couples remained together despite their increasing unhappiness. So Gottman's group designed another experiment in which seventy-nine couples had to answer a number of questionnaires about different aspects of the marriage, as well as having their interaction videotaped and bodily reactions measured as before. Four years later the team succeeded in seeing ninety-two per cent of these couples again to check out how things had changed in the meantime. Even watching the video recordings of the initial interviews again, with the sound turned off, revealed that there had been a number of simple clues about which couples were going to separate. In such couples the wives showed more expressions of disgust (this was the best predictor of all) and the husbands more expressions of fear. Both showed more forced, miserable smiles. In the interaction, both spouses were more defensive, making excuses and denying responsibility; wives complained and criticised more and husbands disagreed more often. When in addition to this the wife openly expressed contempt, and the husband stonewalled as already described, divorce could confidently be predicted.

How reliable were these early-warning signs of

eventual marital break-up? Gottman found that using the signs mentioned above, they could make predictions as to whether couples would separate or stay together which were correct ninety per cent of the time. Besides this astonishing accuracy, there were some other interesting conclusions. As one might expect, husbands who stonewalled were lonely, but they were also discovered to have suffered a deterioration in their physical health over the four years between the first and second assessments. And feminists will be pleased to learn that in those husbands who did housework, physical health improved. They had lower heart-rates than men who did no housework, and were less likely to be overwhelmed by their wives' emotions or to avoid conflict with them. Of course, just what the connections are between all these facts remains to be discovered. It probably all expresses similar conclusions to the known research on healthy families, namely that mental health, and physical health, and good relationships and happy marriages all go together.

Gottman and his team are continuing to explore what makes marriages fail, but are also turning their attention towards what strengthens the bonds and increases the satisfaction between couples. They will next be examining marital interaction at different stages of the life-cycle and making further measurements of the connection between emotions and health. One new approach, no doubt to catch marriages before trouble has had much chance to begin, is a laboratory they are building where newly-weds will be observed continuously over a thirty-five-hour weekend. Here they hope in particular to observe and understand the role of positive emotions in building relationships.

Reflecting on their findings, Gottman admits that the early warning signs that accurately predicted separation later on were perhaps just evidence that the separating process had already started. So how does that begin, and is it reversible once begun? His view is that the separating couples were more defensive and had diminished contact because the interaction felt too painful, so that they began to live parallel lives which no longer touched at a deep emotional level. These results certainly fit well with my own experience of working with couples whose marriages are breaking down. I have been struck for many years by a frequent pattern where the wife is angry and dissatisfied and the husband deals with this by emotional withdrawal and 'stonewalling' in the way the experimenters describe. The man claims he 'can't understand why she is so upset', is 'trying to keep the peace' and 'just wants a quiet life', all of which leaves her with all the responsibility for solving the problem but with no means of exploring how to do so. It is understandable that she becomes increasingly furious and dissatisfied, 73 until she finally gives up and withdraws as well – the beginning of the end. However, if a therapist or counsellor can bring this conflict out into the open and provide a safe arena where both partners are helped to fight their corner without withdrawing, then in many cases the destructive withdrawal can be reversed and, after a very painful period of more open conflict, positive feelings eventually appear.

Marriages of Violence

A common type of troubled marriage is one where the husband withdraws emotionally and 'stonewalls' in the face of his wife's increasing frustration and anger. This sure recipe for marital dissatisfaction often ends with separation and divorce. But some marriages show a reverse pattern, where the husband repeatedly assaults his wife physically while she seems unable to protect herself by leaving him. What is really happening between these couples? In recent years this question could be relied upon to arouse fierce and indeed violent disagreement among many professionals.

The main argument has been between two groups. On the one hand were those who accepted a 'systemic' view of families. This means that blame of any one member is avoided and the complaints and symptoms for which families seek help are assumed to be an unwitting collaboration of all family members in some joint action to solve a deeper problem. In other words, the symptom is an attempted solution, but one that is not working.

This approach has been enormously effective and both speeded up and widened the range of family therapy, as I can testify from my own experience.

As might be expected, professionals who are strongly feminist have balked at the idea that battered wives are collaborating in their victimisation to help the family as a whole, and have bitterly attacked the systemic approach. They feel that the man is simply abusing his unequal power, should be held completely responsible and punished. But in an issue of the journal *Family Process*, four outstanding women therapists at the Ackerman Institute in New York, a leading centre of family therapy and training, report on a series of marriages they treated in which the husband had repeatedly been violent to his wife, and where the team, all with feminist loyalties but also espousing a systemic approach, sought a deeper explanation which would respect both points of view.

In marriages marred by male violence, they found that both partners had grown up in families governed by extreme 'me Tarzan, you Jane' gender stereotypes. Fathers had typically been macho and critical of any sign of tenderness and sensitivity in a boy, regarding it as weakness and 'femininity'. The son would identify with his father's macho attitudes, hide his more vulnerable feelings from him and end up hiding them even from himself. However, he would also feel sympathy for and covertly support his down-trodden mother. When the boy grows up and marries, his feelings towards his wife are influenced by both these loyalties. Provided she keeps to her submissive role he will tend to put her on a pedestal, idealising her and feeling protective as he did with his mother. But if this Tarzan/Jane relationship is threatened by some loss of confidence on his part, or by the woman becoming more independent and assertive, the fears of weakness and dependency he imbibed from his father are re-aroused. Then his father's values take over and bring about desperate attempts to prove to himself that he is a real man, to restore a sense of clear gender difference. This is when the episode of violence usually occurs.

The team also sought to understand the woman's side of the interaction. They refused to accept previous views either that the wife is equally responsible for the violence – 'masochistic', 'asking for it' – or the extreme feminist position that she is an innocent victim whose own actions have no connection whatever with the husband's violent behaviour. In particular, they wanted to understand why these couples seemed so tightly bound and resistant to efforts by professionals to help them separate. Why didn't the wives leave? And why did they seem so ready to engage in the arguments that often led to violence, even sometimes to cast the first stone? What they found came as a surprise. The women were far from being the passive, fearful victims they had been led to expect, and in nearly every case proved to be strong and determined personalities with forceful opinions of their own. Their fierce commitment to the painful relationship with their spouses arose from the values they had absorbed from their mothers, where the most important feature of the feminine role was viewed as the capacity for caring and commitment, and understanding of others. They had married their partners because they sensed their underlying vulnerability and neediness, and felt they could heal them.

This was often a clear motive in the husbands' choice of them as partners. They had sensed that their wives genuinely understood them, accepted the 'weaknesses' their fathers had condemned, and loved them for what they really were. So in the better moments of the relationship they felt more able to be themselves, without keeping up an act. The wives also felt accepted in a way they had never experienced in the families they grew up in, and had been grateful that their husbands admired and approved of their independent strivings – or admired them at least until they began to threaten the man's own confidence. In private and within limits, there could be understanding and acceptance of each other's hidden and denied side: of the man's dependence and of the woman's

assertiveness and desire for equality.

Thus, both members of the couple married because the relationship seemed to offer an escape from the restrictive, rigid, gender stereotypes of the families they grew up in. It promised deeper intimacy, a less extreme polarisation, a possibility of growth and greater fulfilment. In between the violent episodes, this hope was maintained, and it formed the basis of a powerful alliance, a secret coalition which was not disclosed to outsiders. In a sense, it looked like a perfect match.

Now because the relationship is based on an alliance to escape the values of the family they grew up in, things tend to go wrong if this balance of 'the two of us against our families' is upset, either by spouses getting on worse with each other or getting on too well with their families. One of the most inflammatory events, the researchers found, was criticism by one partner of the other's family, since it brought about both these results at the same time.

One great advantage this new understanding gives for treating these troubled couples is the very positive light it throws on the underlying motives which brought the couple together and keeps them joined despite the pain and disappointment. The essential motives are good, towards mutual help and growth; the failure is due to a terrible vicious circle which arises from shaky confidence and unrealistic and exaggerated ideas about what the differences between men and women should be. 79

This knowledge in itself can begin to restore confidence and help to break the destructive pattern.

The Generation Gap

Recently in two therapy groups of mine there were interesting conversations about the 'generation gap' between some members and their adult children. One man spoke of the constant arguments that took place between him and his son, and remembered that he and his father had argued incessantly in exactly the same way. Another man in the group, who had reported similar arguments with his own son, asked 'Have you *told* your son that you did the same thing with your own father?' The first man said he had not, but could not explain why.

It was soon clear that this kind of inhibition was widely shared, not just by people in therapy but by great numbers of ordinary families. Perhaps a majority of parents hesitate to reveal to their children details of their own failings in childhood, believing that they would thereby be failing to set a good example, might lose respect and influence and in some way let their children down. Yet most of us have stumbled on bits of information about our parents' early scrapes and difficulties, often through stories told by grandparents or family friends, and in my experience it often makes them more real and human to us. We warm to them and our respect, and their influence over us, is if anything increased. Also, the standards they set may seem discouragingly beyond our reach as long as their limitations are concealed and they try to appear more perfect than they are; but the imperfect truth may seem more attainable and worth striving for.

As long as this communication between the generations is blocked, we get locked into generational roles, child or parent, whatever our age. Life becomes like a relay race where the baton is not passed on until the first runner drops. Younger people are unable to move on to find a full adult identity until the older generation dies. The barrier prevents real openness and friendship between parents and their adult children, and deprives both of much mutual warmth and support they could otherwise enjoy.

Though this 'Iron Curtain' between parents and their children became increasingly obvious once I began seeing families together, I think I first became aware of it more through the way it affected the work of my profession. I was always puzzled by the awkwardness I felt, when practising as a psychiatrist, at revealing anything at all about my personal feelings or private life, even simple things that members of other professions would use as small talk at the beginning of an interview to break the ice and put the client at ease. There are of course good reasons for not saying too much, because the patient's fantasies about the therapist will then be influenced more strongly by the expectations he or she brings to the session. How the patient treats the therapist will then usually provide important clues about their early family experience. But my own discomfort, and the extraordinary fuss that many of my psychoanalyst and psychotherapist colleagues made about the matter, seemed quite out of proportion and the exploration of this issue became one of my central interests.

Gradually it became clear that this rigid barrier that professionals felt they should draw between their own lives and that of their patients was similar to the 'generation gap' I was observing in the families I have just described. But what was the cause of it? Moving back and forth between first the conventional therapy of individuals and group therapy where I felt most strongly the strange prohibition against personal revelations, secondly family therapy where my colleagues and I seemed for some reason able to be vastly more natural and spontaneous, and thirdly the study of professional teaching institutions where a similar barrier appeared again between the student and the teacher

83

or supervisor, the pattern finally began to make some sense. We seemed to be repeating, in our professional behaviour, the attitude of avoidance and denial that underlies so many of the problems of the people who come to us for help.

The way this works in the families of patients is that the parents have missed out on some support or help they needed in their own childhood, which has left them unable to deal easily with some aspects of life. They have been persuaded that their parents have not failed them in any way, and that any problems they may think they have do not really exist, or if they exist are entirely their own fault and nothing to do with the family. Believing this to be true, they fail to seek out the kind of experience their parents could not give them from some other source, and so do not make good the deprivation in the way that more healthy people do. When they marry and have children, this pattern of deprivation repeats. Instead of accepting to be, in Winnicott's lovely phrase, 'good-enough parents' they try too hard, conceal their own needs and limitations, and present to their children the same impossibly perfect model they received from their own mother and father. The children are then in a double-bind. They sense their parents' neediness and see their inconsistency, but cannot recognise it openly without hurting their parents by making them feel even more inadequate than they do

84

already, and risking losing in the process what limited real affection the parents have received and can pass on. Unless this generation barrier is removed and communication opened up, as it is in family therapy, the pattern can repeat indefinitely.

I believe the same personal dynamics and family pattern underlie the therapist/patient barrier. Everyone loses by it. The patient does not get a real adult model and stays locked into the patient/child role. And like the deprived parents, the therapists suffer too, denying their own problems and seeing these instead in their patients, while giving to them what they really need themselves. It is not surprising that both parties find it hard to stop, and that therapy goes on longer and longer.

However, once parents and children, and patients and therapists, can communicate freely and learn from one another – while retaining respect for real authority based on knowledge and experience – a quite extraordinary chain-reaction of learning can ensue. In family life, treatment situations and teaching institutions, a process of growth develops in which all can share. Having spent much of my life in all three of these, trying to open up communication between them all as widely as possible (experiences brought together in my book *Institutes and How to Survive Them*), I have much reason to be grateful for the benefits it has given.

Can We Become Happier?

*O*ne thing everyone can agree about, I am sure, is that we would all like to be *happy*. But would we actually choose to improve our level of happiness if we got the chance? A professional lifetime of experience as a psychotherapist looking at other people, together with most of a lifetime noting my own reactions as a human guinea pig, tells me otherwise. I have come to believe that in psychotherapy, or in ordinary life, nothing stands in the way of improvement in our functioning so much as the fear of happiness. It is the main reason why therapy takes so long. Let me unpack this statement a bit, for to some people it may come as a surprise.

The first reason is that when we are unhappy – whether we are chronically jealous, or resentful, or depressed or just pessimistic – we know where we are. Horrible though the world may be, there is a wonderful sense of security and predictability about it. We know more or less what will happen tomorrow, because our mood and attitude will make sure that it is very much the same as today.

We are prepared; we are not taken by surprise. And though we live in a perpetual state of dissatisfaction and disappointment, others cannot disappoint us because we have staged a pre-emptive strike by creating a general feeling of disappointment ourselves. It is all under *our* control. No one else can do it *to* us. And anyway, we know the world *is* a disappointing place, because that is how we have always experienced it, because, of course, that is the only aspect of the world we have allowed ourselves to encounter. Like the man in the Guinness advert, as far as any new experience is concerned, we 'haven't tried it because we don't like it'.

The only time I tried skiing I joined the class two days late, after everyone else had learned to stop. So I never mastered this very necessary detail, and when at the end they took us right up the mountain and gave us a shove, the only way I could reduce speed when it reached what felt like eighty miles an hour was to fall over deliberately. This was not at all how I had pictured myself appearing later when showing my holiday snaps to admiring friends, and after a few falls I took off the skis, walked down, and decided to take up some less alarming and exhausting sport. I mention this because the situation is very much the same with the experience of accelerating happiness. Just as negative emotions – the various forms of unhappiness – keep us safely tethered in a secure and known world, happiness is 87 at first terrifying. The mood is confident, accepting, even expansive, exuberant. You readily throw yourself into new experiences and relationships. Worse, once one begins to look as if one is enjoying oneself, other people respond and new relationships and opportunities seem to appear from nowhere. Increasingly, the world seems to be gathering speed at an alarming rate, threatening an excess of pleasure one is not sure one knows how to handle. Like me on the mountain, the only safe thing to do is to fall over. Better to bring the new experience to an end now, than face a more devastating come-down later.

In marital therapy, one sees this pattern for quite some time after a couple achieve a real improvement in their relationship. They will report a dramatic change in their ability to be more loving to one another, and then, inexplicably, out of the blue, return to an episode of violent quarrelling where they seem as alienated as ever, as if the improvement had never happened. It was not until I saw this pattern of anxiety-reducing sabotage in my own marriage each time our relationship improved and became closer, that I recognised it in others. Before this I had always looked for some external cause of the worsening in relationship, and was often mystified because the deterioration was so unexpected and inexplicable. But the cause, I finally had to accept, is simply the fear of happiness.

To accept being happier where one has previously inhabited some chronic negative state also
has profound implications for all one's relationships. At the simplest level, those conversations in
the bus queue which go, 'Awful weather we're
having' . . . 'Yes, isn't it dreadful, never seems to
improve', become less easy. To say, 'Well, actually,
I enjoy it whatever it's like' is unlikely to be well
received, for it destroys the social cement that such
mutual commiseration provides. To be happier is
like moving to another country, where the social
customs and language have to be re-learned.

In any case, most of one's close relationships have
developed on the basis of the kind of person one is –
or, if one is now happier, was. So if we become
happier, we are likely to end up with a very
different circle of friends. It may even threaten the
relationship with one's spouse if he or she prefers to
go on inhabiting the old unhappier world and the
emotional distance becomes steadily harder to
bridge. To contemplate all this in advance, before
one has even met the people whose company one is
going to enjoy more than those one sees now,
makes one feel as though the world will disinte-
grate if one allows the improvement to continue.
So, understandably, on go the brakes.

Of course, even to think about this possibility
feels unpleasantly disloyal. And this fear that one's
attachments will change is nowhere greater than   89

with one's family. The fear is so powerful because it is a manifestation of love – or at least love as one understands it when one is unhappy. The resistance to change stems from reluctance to be happy while one's family are still unhappy. At this stage in therapy people behave as if they have just tunnelled out of a prison camp and, knowing that they could get away if they go it alone, hesitate and turn back because they cannot bear to leave others behind.

In fact, all these resistances to change stem from a perception of what life will be like *after* changes have taken place, from a position *before* this has happened. And like everything else, this perception is coloured by negative emotion and mostly wrong.

Why Children Steal
From Parents

I have explored some reasons for the difficulty most of us find in letting go of habitual attitudes and emotions, and accepting change towards a higher level of health. But most of the explanations I offered for this fear of greater happiness focused on the psychology of the individual confronted with the choice; now I want to take a wider view to include some of the obstacles presented by the social network in which that person is embedded.

At the time I began working in child psychiatry and psychotherapy, thirty-five years ago, it was widely accepted that when children stole from their parents it was a symptom of emotional deprivation. The child, it was thought, felt unloved and was restoring the balance by appropriating something else of value to the parent concerned, frequently money from mother's handbag. In fact, one could usually make a case for an explanation of this sort, and the most common treatment was essentially based on trying in one way or another to remedy the deprivation; that is, to find ways of making the child feel more loved for itself. Sometimes this sense of being more accepted and valued could be achieved through work with the parents, even quite briefly, so that they could make a fresh start and perhaps reverse a vicious circle of alienation set off through some unintended mistake. Where that was not possible, work with the child by an understanding professional was frequently effective, though perhaps more through the positive relationship achieved than by the clever psychodynamic interventions on which we prided ourselves. But in many cases it was slow and uphill work, usually very expensive by comparison with the amounts disappearing from the handbags, and I never felt satisfied that we'd got the theory right. I don't mean that it wasn't right as far as it went – it was certainly part of the truth – but the results were hit and miss in a way that suggested there was much more we needed to understand.

I'm still surprised at how much easier it was to see the missing aspects once we began working with whole families together. We had been seeing parents and children all along, even if separately for treatment. But once we got them interacting in the same room, so that the same therapist was observing the changes in both parents and children, we were able to see the timing of changes more clearly. And it was not long before I noticed that the stealing stopped not so much when the child became happier, or when the parents showed any marked improvement in affection, as (to my surprise) when there was a different kind of change in the parents: when they stopped worrying so much about whether or not they were doing a good parenting job.

Naturally, this startling observation led to much discussion with the families to try to understand it. And what we repeatedly found was that the parents had themselves suffered emotional deprivation in their childhoods, but had denied, and buried, the consequent feelings of rejection and loss – often because expressing these would have threatened the image their own parents had of themselves – and as a result had ended up with powerful unsatisfied needs they were unable to admit to. No longer capable of feeling this emotional hunger in themselves, they experience it when their own children arrive *as if it is in the children*. And if they are half-way decent people trying to be good parents, as most of them are (you get different types of problem if parents are really malevolent), they try to satisfy these needs where they perceive them to be.

Unfortunately, it can't work, as I have explained before. It is bad enough to be deprived without having to try to give to someone else what you have never received in the first place. At best it is a formula for strain and disappointment, and at worst for envy that you have been obliged to give to others   93 what you want so much yourself, even leading to an impulse to spoil it. Inevitably, the children don't get a relaxed, warm sense of being accepted and enjoyed for what they are. Instead, they pick up two contradictory messages at an emotional level: first, that the parents desperately want them to confirm that they are doing a wonderful parenting job; and second, that the parents know they are not in fact giving them enough and feel they should be giving more. Small wonder that the children take this as a cue for them to help balance the books and put things right, by taking an extra helping of something else the parents regard as valuable and actually have available to give – the money in mother's handbag.

In the family interviews, the change for the better comes when, at an appropriate time, this pattern is made known to all. The parents are freed to be aware that they did not feel truly loved as children either, and having been failed themselves, have in this respect failed their children, too, despite all their efforts to do things differently. They see that their parents were probably caught in the same dilemma, and no doubt their grandparents as well, as the pattern repeated down the generations. This is a moment of profound grief, the grief they could not show to their own parents and have kept at bay all their lives. It is also a profoundly moving moment for those who are privileged to witness it.

But it is still not as moving as what usually happens next, as they discover that even in the acknowledgement and acceptance of their deprivation it begins to be repaired, just by being exposed. Frequently the parents become more open and able to give to one another. And now realising that they have burdened their children with their own demands and expectations, they are able both to give more in the sense of a real relationship – even if it seems less than the impossible ideal they were attempting unsuccessfully before – and also to make reasonable demands and set tough limits when necessary, for example over stealing.

It is at this point that the stealing stops. In addition, it is often the child who was referred as 'the problem' who now plays a major part in remedying the parents' deprivation. One fourteen-year-old girl, a family scapegoat who had been in trouble and in therapy of one kind or another from the age of two, and her mother who had a long history of hospitalisation for depression and suicidal attempts, both developed a deeply loving and mutually supportive relationship in the fourth family session, when the family deprivation was finally acknowledged. Over at least the next seven years for which we followed their progress, the girl's misbehaviour ceased and the mother did not need hospitalisation again.

Knowing One's Place

I n *Families and How to Survive Them* John Cleese and I tried to convey how a child in a healthy family develops increasing social competence, and used the image of the child drawing an increasingly accurate map as more and more truthful informa- tion is gathered about the feelings and relationships of others. Exploring the implications of this meta- phor, I vividly remember a momentary sense of shock as I realised that for the mental map to be an accurate guide to life, one had to be represented on it oneself. To be mentally healthy, we need to see ourselves in our right place, and at our right size in relation to everyone else.

Why the sense of shock? I think I was just experiencing an echo of the process we were trying to describe by this image, whereby we all begin as the centre of our personal universe and have to undergo a long series of assaults upon this initial grandiose view of ourselves. It is not so bad having to share the world with mother, because she seems to recognise how enormously important we are, at least when we first arrive. But even she seems not to understand that we need her to be available all the time, and before long there's another major jolt as we discover father and realise to our chagrin that he has priority even with her. As if that isn't enough, other babies arrive uninvited on the scene, and even if we are still the biggest at home we soon find ourselves the smallest at school, and then the smallest at the senior school, and after that the most junior member at work. At each new stage we find our former view of ourselves shrinking, see ourselves as a smaller and more vulnerable part of an ever-larger and more powerful social system. It may all be very good for us, but ouch! it hurts.

To the extent that we can accept and allow these painful experiences to change us, they are not only good for us but also good for everyone else. We come to see ourselves as we are, and see that human nature is pretty constant – that we are basically very much the same as other people despite differences due to upbringing and opportunity. And in seeing our faults and virtues as part of the human condition we become able to accept others, too, can love our neighbours 'as ourselves' because we see that in a deep sense they *are* us – are essentially the same as us. Once we perceive others in this way, fellow-feeling is natural and compassion and consideration tend to follow automatically. 'Society' is then reliably bound together by this network of fellow feeling and understanding, with little need for coercion and threats of punishment.

However, for most of us this painful facing of our limitations is probably only possible as long as the loss of our original sense of omnipotence is compensated by a strong sense of affection, support and security. The toddler is shown that it is still loved, despite its distress and jealousy over the arrival of the new baby; the anxious child attending the new school is buoyed up by the feeling of affection and encouragement it brought with it from home. Where this compensation is lacking, the sense of shrinking self-importance is less readily endured. Instead of seeing ourselves clearly marked on our own mental map, the right size and in the right place, we preserve in fantasy some aspects of our original grandiose self-image. Failing to accept our faults and limitations as part of ourselves, we now see them in other people instead. Since they seem to have these faults while we do not, they appear clearly inferior, while we are clearly superior. And if we believe that we have overcome the faults while they still have them, then they must surely also be to blame for their condition.

Once this false sense of difference and division has developed in a family or a society, many adverse consequences follow. In a family, the negative qualities the parents have not faced are projected into the children, who are genuinely perceived as if they possess them. A child may then sense that it performs a vital function for everyone by allowing itself to be used as a safety-valve for expressing unaccepted family emotions. And, eventually, the dog that is given a bad name begins to live up to it, much as suspects will sometimes make a false confession to escape further harassment.

Just as a child may be cast in, and take on, this dustbin role for its family, so families or communities can play the same part for a whole society. Currently there is much in the news about neighbourhoods where there is a high incidence of stealing cars for joy-riding or ram-raiding of shops, of drug abuse and provocation of the police or of any service identified with central authority. There are two main views about the cause. The first is that these people are different, inferior, not like the rest of us, and that we need to exercise tighter control through tougher policing. The second view is that their behaviour is a consequence of material deprivation and can be remedied by improved material conditions.

I believe neither of these views is adequate. The 'underclass' is just a reflection of the attitudes and values of the rest of society, though being cast in the role of 'have-nots' rather than 'haves', through high levels of unemployment, their options are necessarily different. In joy-riding are they not aspiring, 99 as the television commercials urge us, to the excitement of driving fast, expensive cars? In ram-raiding are they not complying with the pressures of other commercials praising the delights of televisions, hifi's and other electronic wonders?

I am not condoning these actions at all, only suggesting that the lawless and the law-abiding are mostly operating by the same principles, except that some can pay and others can't. They cannot pay because they do not have work, and they do not have work because the majority of us, who are in work, do not want to share it because that would mean sharing the pay, which would make it more difficult for *us* to have the cars and televisions and hi-fi's to which they are helping themselves. As long as we can blame the 'underclass' for their selfish, greedy, materialistic values, we won't need to face the painful truth that we share these, too. And they, blaming us for holding on to our advantages, will be able to continue their sport with a reasonably clear conscience.

Successful Couples

*I*t is extraordinary that there have been no studies of particularly successful marriages, except almost as an aside in accounts of very healthy families, and even then without much depth. Our idea of successful marriage remains a myth, a mirage, the piece of the fairy tale we are never told about, after the last page where the prince and princess marry and live happily ever after.

Instead there is a morbid interest in pathology, unhappiness, failure and betrayal, particularly when it affects couples blessed by affluence or power, and above all, of course, *real* princes and princesses. So the tabloids fill in this gap in our knowledge and do so not with information that might help us to see what underpins success in relationships, which we might draw upon beneficially through positive envy – admiration and the wish to emulate – but in ways that boost self-esteem temporarily through destructive envy. By seeing that someone else, whom we thought more fortunate, is having an even more unpleasant time than we are, even our own failures seem diminished and we can feel superior for a while. But overall our awareness of failure and misery in the world is increased and, in the long run, the more we feed on this evil pap the more our own chances of achieving greater happiness are reduced.

However, the good news is that *We Two*, something in the nature of a first pilot study of successful marriages, has now appeared, and for those who sense that relationships can and should become steadily richer and more fulfilling throughout a lifetime, it is the most valuable guide I have so far encountered. Better still, it is not a 'blue-sky', 'how-to' book but a set of stories in which each member of eight couples separately gives an account of their relationship.

The warmth and affection and tenderness between these couples, the fierce challenge and confrontation and occasional fears that everything may be lost, yet has to be risked, and the excitement and sexual delight and fun, are shared so openly and generously with us, reflecting these vital qualities in their relationship, that one is given at least a taste of the experience itself. It is a book that warms you, cheers you, makes you feel better about the world. Even the photographs of each couple are remarkably moving in their openness and vulnerability as for a moment they trust us, as they trust each other, with the childlike selves we normally cover and protect in public. I still find myself smiling warmly when I remember them.

The editors of *We Two* are Roger Housden and Chloe Goodchild, who run The Open Gate which provides courses and journeys concerned with psychological and spiritual exploration and growth. They began with the question: 'How do couples manage a successful relationship in a culture where there is such disillusion and suffering associated with intimacy, and such confusion over the questions of male and female roles, commitment, child-rearing, fidelity, and the nature and value of love itself?' And chose from among people known to them couples who appeared to have built relationships that worked particularly well.

Not surprisingly the editors have selected couples who are involved, like themselves, in some form of psychological exploration on a professional basis, often in leading roles in organisations they have set up, and working together in some way. This has the advantage that the participants are more aware of what has helped them to build the relationship and to convey it to us, especially as many are talented writers. But it also has the disadvantage that some accounts are obscured by the writers' use of psychological jargon familiar to them but not necessarily to others. However, most stories – and they are the more useful ones – use   103 language that is absolutely direct and simple, and often movingly beautiful.

Some critics will see this bias in the initial selection as invalidating many conclusions that might be drawn from these experiences. Of course it limits the value of the information, and needs supplementing by studies drawn from a wider range of occupations. But you have to start somewhere, and I am reassured by the way that everything that emerges from these accounts fits so well with the research I know on healthy families, with my clinical experience of what helps couples to solve problems and build better relationships, and with my personal experience, too.

The couples are all in their forties and upwards, all very different in personality and in the details of their relationship, though interesting common features emerge from the accounts of their lives together. The first striking fact is that most of them have been married before, and many have children by previous marriages. Yet they agree that successful relationships are highly committed; monogamy is considered important by all, but the commitment is not from moral principle or fear of loss but from choice, from recognising, sometimes through past infidelities, that the high level of pleasure in the interaction is reduced by diluting it. As the actor Paul Newman said when asked why he was so committed to his wife, Joanne Woodward: 'Why

104

have hamburger out when you can have steak at home?'

Some couples have married, though usually for practical reasons. Others have so far decided against formal marriage, feeling their real commitment would be reduced by a contract and preferring instead to recommit themselves continually. The oldest of the couples, now in their sixties, decided quite recently that 'The marriage is the cuckoo in the nest.' So they agreed to dissolve it – though by joint decision, not legally – and say that 'Now, although we have agreed to have no marriage, we seem to have the strongest of marriages.'

Other questions explored by all the couples include: the role of sexuality (vital to them all and increasingly enjoyable; the poem 'Act of Love' by one partner is worth buying the book for); handling jealousy and betrayal (stimulating and highly growth-promoting – if you can stand it); handling conflict (ditto); what makes the relationship alive (all the above, and generally being open, engaged, and vulnerable, feeling oneself and the relationship to be constantly at risk); their experience of love, of the spiritual dimension and the effect of previous marriages and children (all wonderful stuff).

There are so many good things in this lovely book. Do read it. You will be richer for life.

Adjusting Isn't Easy

*D*eveloping a good relationship is a process of mutual adjustment. That's obvious, isn't it? Partners need to give and take, make allowances, find compromises, avoid unnecessary confrontations, try to be reasonable. Surely that's the very least that's required for success.

Well, *is* it? Just try a bit of this adjusting in the process of walking along a crowded street, attempting to avoid the other passers-by. Where a moment before everyone was effortlessly threading their way through the crowd past you, and you past them, miraculously and without a thought, you start to bump into other people. You try to avoid them, but their guidance system has already calculated the alteration of course needed to avoid *you*, and now your change has put you on a new collision course. Then they see you, begin to make conscious adjustments as well, and you both begin jumping from side to side at an increasing rate like tennis players awaiting a serve. The delay that occurs 106 while each recalculates the other's trajectory ensures that one adjustment cancels out the other, until the impact occurs.

More often to avoid the collision both parties stop dead and wait to see what the other will do. Again there is the same built-in delay on both sides between observation of the other's movements and adjustment to them, so that this little scenario can sometimes be repeated several times before they get past each other and proceed on their way.

Now my experience is that a similar process occurs in families when people worry too much about adjusting to one other. One family came to see me because a twelve-year-old son suffered from colitis. But what came across in the interview was the anxiety all members felt about upsetting or displeasing one another. I enquired what they all did together to enjoy themselves, and asked them to describe, in detail, a recent family decision of this kind. It turned out that each had wanted to do rather different things, but had put others first and yielded to someone else's suggestion. In the end, they had ended choosing something that *no one* had really wanted to do.

Exploring other decisions of this kind, the same pattern emerged each time. It was rare for anyone to get to do what they really enjoyed, and very often they ended up doing nothing at all. Eventually the father, a clergyman, exclaimed, 'Good Heavens! This is charity gone mad!'; as indeed it was – 107 concern for the welfare of others carried to an extreme where it was having the opposite effect to that intended.

At the next interview, they reported a change in the way they came to such decisions. Each would now state their preference firmly and enthusiastically, and sustain their position in the ensuing discussion. Instead of a compromise which was unsatisfactory for everyone, based on trying to avoid making others *unhappy*, they focused on making at least one person *happy*. It often proved that more than one of them enjoyed a particular activity, and those who were less keen on it at least enjoyed the enjoyment of the others – which was what they had been aiming for all along, but previously failing to achieve. And in any case, their turn would come next time. The family looked much more cheerful, and the boy's bowel symptoms steadily improved.

When walking down the street, we relax and walk ahead into the crowd, and either they, or we, automatically move aside. In a sense, each time one 'wins' and the other 'loses'. But there is really no loss if we both get to our destination. And similarly, it seems that a certain kind of 'healthy selfishness' is required for effective decision-making and resolution of conflicts. It enables others to 'know where we stand'; indeed, enables *us* to know where *we* stand, for if we never try to express ourselves clearly we often remain unsure of what we really want. If all parties say what they want, and stand their ground, a decision will be reached which is at least based on the real needs of all involved. Again, some will *give* way, while others will *have* their way, but a result is achieved which at least satisfies someone's desires. And if you feel satisfied, you are more likely to be generous and give way next time to whoever has given way to you.

In marriage in the past, conflict was avoided by the traditional gender power structure. The man stepped off the pavement for the woman, even if he no longer cast his cloak in the puddle to keep her feet dry. And at home, the reverse arrangement applied.

But when the woman demands equality, the man is challenged. If he doesn't accept that he must change himself, he may either continue to try to dominate through economic power or physical strength, less and less an option; or more often withdraw and withhold support and affection, an increasingly frequent cause of marital break-up, because the woman eventually decides that she is still getting a raw deal, even if a different one. A third possibility is complete capitulation, but this is the old hierarchy turned upside down, with all the old disadvantages and some new ones as well.

The fourth option, of course, is for the man to accept the need to grow as the woman has grown, and engage more fully. This brings challenge and struggle; but so do football, tennis, and other enjoyable sports. As someone expressed it in *We Two*, 'Excitement, life, lies in the difference, the difficulty of living with someone so different, who does not hide it.' It also brings personal growth. In *We Two*, the male partner of another couple said, 'Being committed to growth and personal development is the "diamond-cutting" phenomenon. It takes one hard diamond to shape and cut another . . . It takes the hassles of being in the presence of an unrelenting and loving other to make one see the need to shape up.'

But for this to be possible, even enjoyable, affection is vital. As this man's partner put it: 'The new spaces opening in me . . . have flowered in response to Z's presence in my life . . . He has made space for me to expand, to risk, to try new and unfamiliar things . . . Perhaps I had never realised before what I had to give . . . There is something about being so warmly *loved* that supports and frees me to discover who I am and who I might become . . . It is in the flow of my love for him that I am carried a little beyond myself . . . I am fully involved, and therefore fully at risk.'

'Sealed Orders' in the Family

I have written about the expectations society has had of men in the past, and the difficulty men have had in adjusting to the changing roles of women because neither the original expectations, nor the new requirements, have been properly explored and made explicit. And I have described the liberating experience of sharing this question with a group of men where gaining a clearer awareness of the issues was like suddenly being freed from a magic spell. I had not been able to escape from the spell before because I was completely unaware of being in its power. But once these expectations were recognised and named I felt instantly freed to consider the possibility of changing to other patterns of behaviour.

This is just an example of how, in childhood, we absorb a complex pattern of rules, pressures and taboos while remaining hardly conscious of the process. We may be aware of fragments of this conditioning which are conveyed in words – 'Big boys don't cry', 'Little girls are made of sugar and

spice and all things nice' – but most of the instructions are conveyed by subtle non-verbal signals, or
by imitation, and we are conscious neither of the
scope and detail of the instruction book our parents
have given us, or that all the different rules,
exhortations and prohibitions make up a closely
linked system, each part of which reinforces the rest
and cannot be changed without a major revision.
And a major revision is impossible, of course, until
we realise what it is that is creating problems for us,
and that it *can* be changed.

In other words, we start life like a captain setting
sail with sealed orders, unaware of where he is
going, or why. But the difference is that the captain,
once at sea, does get to discover what the orders are
and has some choice about whether to carry them
out, or at least can alter details in the light of
changing circumstances. While we, thinking ourselves to be masters of our fate and captains of our
souls, never get to know what the orders were
because they go straight to the steersman and
engine-room; that is to say, most of our social
training, including our religious views, moral
standards and emotional imperatives and inhibitions, takes place below the level of consciousness.

In fact, escape from this conditioning is made
even more difficult by certain sealed orders which
are instructions about how to deal with the sealed
112 orders themselves. One of these states that the

sealed orders shouldn't be opened or, if accidentally opened, should not be taken seriously or discussed with others but quickly put back in the envelope and forgotten. However can we know we shouldn't open the orders, you may ask, if we haven't opened them already? Remember that the orders are all being received and acted upon below the level of consciousness; the prohibition is about our *conscious awareness* of them. And as long as we are not consciously aware of them we cannot question them, and have to take our family belief-system for granted.

A second sealed order states that all the family rules, taboos, religious beliefs and moral imperatives are not only healthy, but if anything *healthier* than those of other families. So even if we become aware of them, they will seem natural and right and it will feel wrong to change them.

A third order is about avoiding contact with other people who are operating under sealed orders very different from our own. We cannot even entertain the idea of changing anything until we encounter something different and realise there is an alternative. So families which cannot tolerate change and independence in their members have rules which restrict their experience of the wider world. Children will be discouraged from contact with other families. In the sickest families playmates may be completely discouraged, while more ordinary 113 families may deter friendships with children from other social classes and religious backgrounds, or with different manners and values. By depriving us of information about alternative views of the world and the different possibilities of development open to us, these three 'orders about the orders' inevitably restrict change and threaten to stunt our growth.

Is there a way out? There is once we begin to understand our situation in the way I have just described it. The great majority of families consciously desire and seek the happiness and well-being of everyone in them; the problem is that all members, parents and grandparents included, are operating blindly and automatically under the same sealed orders, including the three 'orders about the orders' mentioned above which make exploration and change so difficult. At the same time, the surrounding social world is bombarding us with information which could set us free. Whatever limitations, prejudices and taboos our families suffer from they are constantly being challenged through our contacts with neighbours, at school and work, and through newspapers, magazines, books, theatre, films, radio, television and foreign travel. These two opposing pressures, from the familiar world of our intimates and the unfamiliar world beyond, are constantly playing upon us; and

whether we remain fixed and limited all our lives, or

change and grow, depends upon the balance reached between them.

If we want to change this balance we must first escape from the three 'orders about the orders'. The first of these has trained us not to see – that is to deny – certain emotions or family patterns; and though we cannot hope to see easily what we have been trained *not* to see, we have more chance of doing so if we at least know that our vision is distorted. The second rule has defined our family values as more healthy than those of others; and if we know this is less than the truth we will be more likely to recognise, and be able to emulate, greater health when we encounter it. But it is the third rule – the one which restricts our contact with people who hold views different from those of our own family – which we can challenge most easily. If we consciously and consistently struggle against this one rule, and take as many opportunities as possible to expand our lives to include new and unfamiliar contacts and experience, particularly those we shrink from because they make us feel uncomfortable, we will give ourselves the best possible chance of new learning and positive change.

Sex, Education and the Small Screen

S ome time ago Channel 4 screened a programme in which a panel had reviewed a range of the new sex education videotapes and announced their first four choices. For those who missed this useful guide, these were: *Lover's Guide 2*; *Making Love*; *Better Sex*; and *Super Virility*. These were considered not only the most helpful but also the most arousing.

But should they *be* arousing? A controversy continues about whether such videos are valuable educational resources which should be freely available at our friendly neighbourhood bookstore, as at present, or pornography in disguise, requiring control. The survey had not put these four videos in any particular order, so I chose *Lover's Guide 2* because I had already been much impressed by Dr Stanway's writings. I should emphasise that I have only seen the clips of the alternative recommendations that were shown as part of the survey mentioned, and have no reason to suppose that they differ in usefulness.

116　　Until my recent retirement from practice I had

been dealing for twenty years mainly with marital problems, usually requiring some focus on the sexual relationship, and had in the past seen not only pornographic movies but many videos of all kinds of sexual activity as part of attending or providing sex education courses for professionals. But the explicitness of *Lover's Guide 2* came as a shock, even to me. By this I don't mean that I disapproved or found it unpleasant; quite the reverse. It was simply a surprise – and a very pleasurable surprise – to find sex described and demonstrated with such complete openness and naturalness, in a way that captured the sense of pleasure and fun yet also felt absolutely wholesome and healthy.

The main reason is the choice of couples. They are (or certainly give the impression of being) in caring and committed relationships, relaxed and at ease in this most intimate of relationships, and conveying in their physical contact strong feelings of tenderness and affection. At times they have been helped to forget the camera sufficiently for normal fun and mischief to bubble up. I found myself smiling warmly, because it was just so lovely.

This relaxed atmosphere is clearly facilitated by Dr Stanway, whose easy, relaxed commentary – matter-of-fact, light yet serious – counteracts any embarrassment due to one's inevitable feeling of voyeurism. He is like a physicist at one of those

Christmas scientific lectures for children, enthusiastically demonstrating the fascinating changes of
colour obtained by mixing chemicals, a television
gardener showing us how to grow more beautiful
flowers, a television cook helping us to prepare the
most delicious dishes. Simmer gently for forty-five
minutes, adding as many spices as you can find;
then turn the gas right up, stirring briskly, until it all
boils over completely.

One criticism I have heard is that the couples are
mostly young and attractive and older people are
under-represented. This is true, but since older
people will have grown up in a time of greater
sexual prudishness and inhibition, their needs may
require somewhat different treatment. I imagine
that such videos are being made, if they do not exist
already, but I believe any reasonably normal couple
of any age (up to seventy at any rate; I can't be
certain what it's like after that) is bound to be helped
to a happier sexual adjustment by a video of this
kind.

Which brings me to ITV's own *Good Sex Guide*,
presently screening on Monday evenings. This has
come in for a bit of a clobbering from the 'some-
people-may-need-it-but-there's-nothing-wrong-
with-me' school of television criticism, but I think
it's just brilliant. It is inevitably less explicit and
detailed than the videos on sale, though a lot more
frank and direct than anything I have seen before on

the main TV channels. But it makes up for this in its presentation. To make themselves acceptable as educational, the videos tend to damp down the excitement with their more serious 'We doctors believe . . .' commentaries. But whatever else sex is, at its best it is raunchy, animal, wild, abandoned, extreme, and above all playful, fun, as well as (whether at the same time, or at other times) tender, gentle, loving, considerate. It is akin to fighting, indeed sometimes develops out of it, and a visiting Martian could be forgiven for assuming it to be a form of combat. I cannot imagine how it could be really good and also restrained, dignified, controlled, though of course a certain self-discipline is necessary as part of it to ensure the maximum pleasure of both. The *Good Sex Guide* solves this problem by carrying the excitement, liveliness and fun in its script, and in the extraordinary performance of its presenter, Margi Clarke. Stunning, enormous fun, yet direct, straightforward, reassuring and natural; the girl next door, or at least the girl we would all have liked to live next door to, she conveys a complete acceptance and enjoyment of her physical being and invites us to enjoy our own. Her remarks are raunchy, often outrageous, but with perfectly timed humour and a total absence of anything offensive.

The fragments of interviews where members of the public answer very frank questions about their sexual lives provide wonderful models of sexual confidence and enjoyment. And the humorous sketches – the international sex Olympics, the penises on parade – are often corny but usually amusing, to me at least, and like the rest of the programme they manage to startle us into a more open-minded acceptance of sex by going just beyond the limits of what we are expecting. The inhibited and inarticulate are admittedly under-represented in the programmes, but other videos can be made focusing on particular problems; indeed, some are already used for sex therapy. And as John Cleese says at the beginning of *Life and How to Survive It*: 'If you want to write a book about how to paint, or play chess, or be a good manager, you'd start by studying the people who are good at those things. And you wouldn't expect heavy sales of a book called *Play Championship Golf by Learning the Secrets of the Worst Twenty Players in the World*.'

So, are these programmes pornographic? I can only speak for what I've seen, but I saw not the slightest sign of it in Stanway's video, and the *Good Sex Guide* is about as far from pornography as you can get. The essence of pornography is the deliberate separation of sex from warm human concern and affection, and the charm of these educational programmes is the way they show these aspects of human nature so completely integrated. It is this model of enjoyment, and combination of warmth and excitement, love and lust, which is the most effective teacher and healer.

Parents, Children and the Sex Taboo

W hy do we so easily become embarrassed about the display of sexual feelings? One major reason is that we get such confused and conflicting messages telling us when we are allowed to show normal sexual responses and when we must pretend this aspect of our being doesn't even exist. But probably the main source of embarrassment is the fact that, by its nature, the sexual relationship sharply excludes others from an experience of intense pleasure which can be enjoyed most fully by just two people. For the moment they are totally absorbed in one another and uninterested in any other relationship, so the event can be expected to arouse intense jealousy and destructive envy in those who become aware that it is happening. The pair involved will experience corresponding fears in return, and therefore a strong desire to conceal the fact that they are having so much more enjoyment than others.

This, I have come to believe, is why we feel such a powerful need to hide this side of life from children. We rationalise this by imagining it may do them harm, and certainly the incestuous breaking of the parent/child sexual boundary, either physically or through an emotional involvement which properly belongs between adults, can destroy trust and violate a child's development. But *knowledge* about the nature of parental love is a different matter; confidence that the parents are happy in their physical relationship is a powerful source of security to children, and the jealousy naturally aroused is one of the most powerful motors propelling us towards growth, emotional separation and independence. The main reason that we fear our ardours may be overheard by our children is because we realise they will sooner or later get fed up with being excluded from these delights and, very sensibly, will leave us in order to find partners of their own and start their own families.

In my experience children – which of course means all of us in our beginnings – know about it anyway. We don't learn about sex; we learn to forget we know because it makes our parents uncomfortable. But if when we become parents we can allow our children to retain this knowledge it can be helpful to us as well as to them.

As one might expect, adolescents and young adults still living with their parents are likely to have the most accurate awareness of their parents' sexual difficulties, though their capacity to 'let themselves know they know' will still be subject to family 123 taboos. The larger the family the more the children are able to support one another in resisting such irrational parental inhibitions and this can work to the parents' advantage when the children's greater openness also helps their father and mother to become less inhibited in communicating with one another about sexual matters.

For example, one difficult couple fought so bitterly during interviews that I asked my wife to join me as co-therapist. But their fiery interaction, though mild enough compared with their home life where he would sometimes come home drunk and break down her bedroom door, defeated our joint efforts to help them pursue a cooperative discussion. Still, it was clear that they both greatly valued their relationships with their children, and as we were at our wits' end we suggested these might join us. To our surprise, the father was delighted, and at the next session there were twelve of us – ourselves, the parents, and eight children ranging in age from early teens to mid-twenties – packed tightly into the room. The father, formerly irascible and provocative, was completely transformed by the presence of his daughters, who clearly loved him and were treated by him with deep respect.

In the presence of the family, the parents were now able to listen to one another as the father expressed his distress at what he saw as the mother's sexual rejection of him, and the mother in

124

turn explained how she could not help withdrawing from him as long as he expressed his needs in a violent and demanding way. The interventions of the children, and the willingness of the parents to heed and be helped by what they said, were immensely moving. At one point a daughter who clearly had great influence with the father told him gently that he didn't understand women – all that shouting and swearing, she said, it wasn't the way to win a woman's affection; father needed to realise that women wanted men to be *nice* to them!

With this support the parents gradually discovered that, underlying their sexual difficulty, they both suffered from similar feelings of deprivation and longing for affection. Their quarrels were not only a demand for this, and a substitute for affectionate forms of intimacy, but also protected them from the vulnerability to which emotional closeness would expose them.

Now that the children were involved, quite extraordinary progress was made towards achieving a happier marriage, at a rate and to a degree we would never have imagined possible while seeing just the parents together.

The Springs of Well-being

What kinds of experience contribute to feelings of well-being? In my books I have explored extensively what kinds of life-conditions, and especially of family-functioning, are generally associated with health and happiness, but have not really investigated the nature and generation of well-being in any great detail until my recent illness and hospitalisation, when I had both a good opportunity and strong incentive to observe the factors which maintain one's good spirits and ability to enjoy life in adverse circumstances.

The principles at work are, of course, operating all the time in daily life and a variety of both cheering and depressing events are constantly raising or lowering our mood. The more we know about these, the more we can regulate our mood ourselves and maintain feelings of well-being and if not elation and happiness at least, perhaps, glimpses of a deep and quiet contentment, even in difficult times.

126 Psychological theories have tended to focus

particularly on negative effects, because of the association with medical concepts of disease, and in general they offer less help towards the maintenance of buoyant mood; so, apart from the 'blue sky' self-help books and many readings aimed essentially at spiritual improvement, there is not much to draw upon. Most of our learning comes from our own experience; and also from the accumulated experience of others, transmitted as folk wisdom or common sense.

The sources of well-being can be divided first into those that come from outside us and those which have their source within. Of those provided by the outside world the most obvious and easily recognised, though not the most important, are inputs of pleasure we can arrange for ourselves. These frequently involve drawing upon material resources of some kind. A treat, like a special meal, an entertainment, a massage, a hairdo, as well as the arrival of a cheque which will make more such treats possible are all 'cheerful' and give us an emotional boost. Our mothers and grandmothers usually tell us that money can't buy happiness. True, but it can buy time, some kinds of security, and also comfortable, attractive surroundings where positive experiences are more easily found or created.

People will differ widely in the extent to which they can afford to arrange these mood-enhancing experiences but some may be able to derive greater benefit from the contact with nature provided by a day in the country, or even in a park, garden or allotment, than those more wealthy can obtain through an expensive purchase or visit to the theatre or opera. Indeed, among a number of very wealthy people I chanced to see in psychotherapeutic practice, happiness was strikingly hard to find.

But the most important inputs, especially in times of hardship or illness, are the affection and support of one's nearest and dearest, from spouse or life-partner and other family members to friends. One's well-being is powerfully enhanced by the well-wishing of others, and it is perhaps only in adversity that one discovers the scale of this warmth and support which must have been potentially available all the time. When in hospital, cut off from one's usual contacts, not only visits but telephone calls and messages, cards and letters from loved ones provide infusions of strength, stamina and a positive mood. Perhaps one's main *inner* resource is at the other end of these connections, the affection we have developed for those who are helping us or wishing us well, and the feelings of gratitude evoked by their kindnesses in the present adverse circumstances. For in adversity, as in good times, it is the love one feels for others rather than the passive enjoyment of being loved which most enhances one's well-being.

If there is any other quality which can sustain us in a comparable way it is the connection with *oneself* – the ability to make and keep contact with the sense of one's inner life – to experience vividly and enjoy the fact and feeling within of being alive. This awareness of the flow of living energies animating us is always potentially available, though we lose it as a result of the myriad distractions which constantly tempt us away from the essential centre of ourselves. But the more we stay in touch with it and seek it again when there is opportunity, the more readily we will find this life-enhancing resource when we need it. And, as with the ability to nurture and sustain our love for others, this capacity to sense vividly the vital core of our being is more available in adversity if we have practised and developed it when there is spare time and energy to do so. More and more people nowadays have drawn on traditional Eastern methods of developing this kind of attention to one's inner life-energies, like different forms of meditation, yoga and Tai Chi, but many still find it through Western religious practice like prayer and retreats. And others come to it through the experience of stillness and quietness induced by contact with nature, poetry, or beauty of other kinds.

Our most pleasurable activities follow this imperative. Any activity practised with a high degree of attention is inherently pleasurable and   129 attractive precisely because it gives us a taste of our inner life, at the same time that it heightens the awareness of what we are attending to. Children are following this principle when they delight in playing games like Hopscotch or throwing balls against a wall to complicated rhythms. And at any age attention-demanding recreations – including team sports or tennis, wind-surfing, fly-fishing, or climbing – are engaged in partly because they make us feel more alive, and so make life feel even more worth living. Those who can bring this kind of attention to their work tasks are especially fortunate because they will not only enjoy life more but also be strikingly successful in their achievements, because work has become as enjoyable as play. And to the extent that this awareness of the life-energies welling up within us becomes more readily available, there are resources of meaning and pleasure at hand in even the most negative circumstances. Lying in a hospital bed, for example, there is nothing to stop one meditating and drawing on this resource as often as one likes.

At times we are more open to some resources than to others. So the order in which we draw upon them may be important. In negative moods we may need to be 'by ourselves' for a time and find a way of getting into a highly attentive state before we can make contact with our positive feelings for others in order to recognise and be supported by theirs for us

– a nugget of folk-wisdom expressed by the old nursery rhyme:

Crosspatch! – shut the latch,
Sit by the fire and spin,
Take a cup and drink it up,
And call the neighbours in.

All in the Mood

*I*n general, our families are systems possessing mechanisms – like the governor on a steam engine or the thermostat on a refrigerator or central heating system, which most of the time maintains the mood of its members within a quite narrow range.

This idea of the family as a self-regulating 'system' is not easy to grasp, as everyone practising family therapy finds whenever they struggle to do so. Sometimes a physical analogy helps. Imagine for a moment a family where cooking together is a valued tradition. Fairness is important to them also, so each family member is allotted one gas ring or the oven to cook one item of the meal. Let us suppose that the youngest family member – let us call him Junior – has just reached the age where he can be trusted to join in this activity. He is asked to cook a vegetable for the Sunday lunch and is allocated a gas ring. Determined to be ready on time, he turns his gas ring on full to make sure the water boils swiftly. But he notices that as he does so the flames on all the other rings become low. He gets high marks for physics at school and quickly reaches the reasonable conclusion that the supply of gas is limited, due to too small a supply pipe perhaps, and that by taking a lot of gas himself he has deprived others of their share. He is left in no doubt about this by the upset and accusatory expressions with which other family members look at him. So he turns his gas low and, seemingly confirming his theory, the other gas rings burn more brightly again.

A few months later the school refers Junior to the local child guidance clinic. The teachers have become worried because he has recently taken to disrupting chemistry classes by turning down the gas supply to other people's Bunsen burners in the middle of their experiments. His explanation for these actions, the head reports, is a strange belief that over-use of the Bunsen burners will cause the central heating systems in the local hospital to fail; so the patients will get chilled, perhaps develop pneumonia, even die.

The child guidance clinic turns out to be using the most up-to-date ideas and methods, including family therapy. They have one-way viewing screens not only onto the usual treatment rooms but also onto the clinic kitchen, so that treatment teams can closely observe the interaction of families around the eating behaviour of anorexic children. Junior and his family are invited to cook a meal in   133 this kitchen and even though it is known that the clinic gas stove has a large supply pipe, big enough to enable all the rings to be operated on full, when Junior turns his gas high, here as at home all the other rings fade and flicker.

However, a member of the viewing team behind the one-way viewing screen provides another possible explanation. She has noticed that every time Junior turns his gas up and his flames leap into the air, the hands of other members of the family move towards their taps. This advanced clinic also has closed-circuit TV and video-recording equipment and repeated viewing of the videotape confirms that each time Junior turns his tap up, all other family members turn theirs down.

The family therapist is informed of this discovery by a message from the team, but before he can make use of it Junior, whose aptitudes have led to his being regarded as the family scientist and mechanic, now inspects the whole stove, looking for a fault which has interrupted the gas supply, and discovers that all the taps except his own are completely turned off. He knows they could not have turned themselves off and that his family must be responsible. He now challenges them to explain this strange behaviour. They all deny responsibility and protest that the only problem is his extravagance with the gas. But Junior's suspicions have been aroused and he decides to experiment by keeping his gas on full, no matter what happens to the rest of the burners.

Freed from his previous preoccupation with adjusting to his family, he now cannot help noticing how the hands of other family members move to their gas taps and turn them down, though they continue to shoot accusatory looks in his direction. He is now rather enjoying himself and turns it all into a game. The others get cross and an argument develops during which he says he is only playing the same game that they have been playing all along; he has simply turned the tables. The therapist encourages this lively, enjoyable interaction: 'Oh, well played. You tricked everyone to turn their gas right off again.' A good time is had by all, Sunday lunches at home are better than ever and ready on time, Junior loses his anxiety about central heating breakdowns and leaves the Bunsen burners alone at school.

A rather fanciful scenario you may be thinking, and I confess that I have never encountered this exact complaint during my professional work. But substitute 'happiness' or 'enjoyment of life' for 'strongly burning gas ring' and I met this scenario every day. Many families have an unspoken rule that no one should be much more happy than anyone else. There is a flat depressive tone about the whole family atmosphere, and if one member is in particularly good spirits everyone else feels worse by contrast. So there is a constant jockeying for position, not so much to have advantage but rather to ensure that no one else has any advantage and that all feel equally miserable. If one family member is in a particularly good mood, others will make comments like: 'Why are *you* looking so pleased with yourself today?' 'It's all right for some, isn't it!' 'You just don't care about me, but you'll be sorry when I've gone'; 'You're getting too excited, dear'; and then, 'It will all end in tears, you know', in a tone betraying the unspoken, 'And don't worry, we'll make sure it does.'

Some families try to control mood in a similar fashion, but to maintain family equality in high rather than low spirits and maintain a constant frisson of excitement. Everyone is expected to be 'bright-eyed and bushy-tailed' all the time and anyone who falls below the standard is subject to pressure to 'buck up', 'wear a smile', and generally perform well to ensure that 'the show must go on'. Children from such families usually cope better with life, but to be truly themselves they too have to see through, and escape from, the family mood-regulating rules.

The Challenge to Men

O ne of the great unexplained mysteries of our time is
the extraordinary delay after the flowering of the
women's movement in the mid-1960s and early 70s
before the male half of the human race has begun to
develop any comparable response to this challenge
which has so profoundly changed much of the
world. Indeed, wonderful creatures that we are, we
men have not shown a lot of awareness that
anything was required of us at all.

My interest in 'family therapy', then regarded as a
revolutionary way of treating emotional problems,
began the year before the publication in 1963 of
Betty Friedan's *The Feminine Mystique*. So the new
ideas that were emerging from feminists about
gender-roles and male/female relationships coin-
cided with the new information I was getting from
families. I have written about how these meetings
with the whole family forced me to revise most of
the ideas I had received during my training and how
it was the children and the mothers who demanded
a tougher, more authoritative attitude on the part of

the father. There is no fury, I found, to match that of a teenage daughter whose father has avoided confrontation and never put his foot down, the final damning evidence, so it seemed, of lack of love and care! I also mentioned the understanding my late wife and I gained from our work with couples' groups, where we encountered a similar demand on the part of the wives for the husbands to find an independent, strong, clear position in relation to them, even at the price of conflict. The main problem was getting the men to do it.

Throughout this period I was therefore getting conflicting messages about some aspects of the role that men needed to play. I had welcomed the new, broader role that women were adopting, accepted the principle of equality in all respects, and have benefited enormously myself from the changes these developments can in turn facilitate in men. But the message of all my professional experience at this time was that men were not, and should not try to be, the same as women, and that in trying to destroy paternal authority, identified so much then with male dominance and violence, we were heading for family break-up and social chaos.

The influence of the women's movement had helped many men to get in touch with their feelings and relate to women more deeply. But in the process they seemed to have lost something essentially male – hard to define but connected with

138

liveliness, assertiveness, clarity, directness. I had developed some gut feelings about the new role that men needed to take but found myself unable to put it clearly into words, or justify it, or communicate it to others except in the actual process of therapy. And until very recently no help seemed to be at hand.

Then, in June 1990, when John Cleese and I addressed the American Family Therapy Association, we found the two other outside speakers were the feminist Susan Griffin and the main leader of the new men's movement in the US, the poet Robert Bly. I had read about Bly in one of the American family therapy journals a few months earlier and been particularly interested in his ideas about the need for men to contact what he called the 'wild man' in themselves, and the 'warrior', a capacity for fierceness in self-defence and defence of the partner and family.

Once one sees him it would be hard to imagine a more appropriate figure to spearhead a development of this kind. Six foot three or four, with the build of a trapper, a mane of white hair, and a stern and fierce visage, he inspires the kind of respect one would give a seemingly friendly polar bear. Yet closer acquaintance revealed great warmth and humour, deep resources of sensitivity and gentleness towards the genuine vulnerabilities of others, and a profound and infectious love of poetry and 139 beauty in all its forms. He is also very funny indeed, and a marvellous entertainer.

Bly found himself in his present role through his own search for what manhood means at this time in Western society, and one of his great merits as a communicator and teacher is the way he shares so freely with others his own earlier problems and confusions as well as his continued questioning and exploration. His influence had already affected the association to which we were all speaking. A strong women's group addressing feminist concerns had existed within it for many years, but this year an additional day had been set aside for a parallel men's group as well. I had signed on for this men's group and was apprehensive that the event might attract either hen-pecked grumblers or tame feminists. But I need not have worried. Many of the thirty men attending were either distinguished senior figures whose work I had long admired or men I had liked the look of and engaged, or wanted to engage, in conversation earlier. Those convening the meeting (there was no formal leader) invited us all to speak and we spent the rest of the morning doing so in turn.

Bly spoke in his talk about the depth of grief he found in most men once they were able to open their hearts, particularly over their feeling that they had never felt a close relationship with their fathers.

140 Though details differed this was entirely confirmed

by what now followed. Many wept, and most, myself included, were profoundly affected by finding echoes in their own experience. The sense of freedom, warmth and acceptance that developed in the room cannot be described. I discovered, as I think we were all discovering, that we no longer felt separated from other men by some failure in that vital early relationship with the father, but united to other men by the sharing of that deficiency and by the beginning realisation that men, together, could remedy it.

Iron John

'Middle-class Males Unite to go Wild'; that was the headline above a recent article about a men's weekend in Texas, which began by describing them as '. . . running, dancing and talking about themselves before being crammed naked, thigh to thigh, inside a giant wigwam . . .' in order to '. . . put men back in touch with the wild man alleged to be inside all males'. This was the first time I had seen the new men's movement in America mentioned in a British newspaper. And this was the *Sunday Times*. I shuddered to think what the *News of the World* or *Sunday Sport* would make of it.

I get six American magazines concerned with family problems and their treatment, but there had been no mention of this strange new development until one had run a feature on it six months earlier. From this, and other American reports I then sought out, I learned that it had been under way for about ten years and that the guiding spirit was Robert Bly, a distinguished American poet in his early sixties who had won the National Book Award

in 1968 and been a prominent opponent of the
Vietnam war. In mid-life, a number of his interests
came together to impel him to explore what men
needed to do to complement the immense changes
that have taken place in women over the last twenty
years. These interests included ancient myths and
fairy tales, and Jungian psychology which draws so
much on mythological material for its understanding of the origins of human conduct. About this
time he was also struggling to understand and come
to terms with his own confusions about the male
role, intensified by the unreliabilities of an alcoholic
father.

He began to share this exploration with other
men at his poetry readings and then in longer
gatherings, discovering in the process that the
sense of disappointment and failure he had felt in
his relationship with his father was not peculiar to
him but very widely experienced. Gradually, it
became clearer that what he had been trying to deal
with was not just a personal problem, but a crucial
failure of our present society to provide certain
experiences that were vital for the healthy development of males. His father's problems, he saw, had
arisen from the same deficiency.

What is missing, Bly believes, is some essential
contact with older men that young males need in
order to develop confidence, strength, and the
ability to enjoy their male energies vigorously, but   143

in the context of a sense of responsibility and service to the whole community. In what we often call 'primitive' societies – but which are often more intelligent and well-ordered than our own – this transition is usually managed by the community with great care through initiation ceremonies. Boys are removed from their families to the company of older men and put through experiences which admit them to membership of the male brotherhood while ensuring that they become aware of their overriding responsibility to the group.

As part of this process in the Kikuyu tribe in Africa, for instance, a boy is taken from his mother to a prepared place away from the village. After fasting for three days he is brought to sit in a circle around the fire with the older men. Each man in turn takes a knife and opens a vein to allow his blood to flow into a bowl as it passes around. Finally the boy is invited to drink from it, as a symbol that he is now one of them and they are committed to his welfare. Even in Western society boys who grew up in the country would, from an early age, spend time alongside their fathers and other men, helping them in their work in the fields. Bly dates the onset of men's present uncertainties about their role to the industrial revolution, when fathers disappeared into factories and offices so that this crucial contact largely ceased.

144   To begin to remedy this, gatherings of men like

those reported in my opening paragraph are taking place all over the US. The total numbers of men involved are still relatively small, no more than about 50,000 by 1990, but most large cities now have at least one group operating, and interest is growing rapidly.

Robert Bly has tried to gather his ideas together and present them in a form which makes them available to a wider public through his recently-published book, *Iron John*. This is centred around a detailed examination of the symbolism contained in an ancient story which forms one of the Grimms' fairy tales. Around this he weaves information and ideas drawn from social studies, depth psychology, anthropology and mythology, together with much detail about his own family background and personal development, the whole enlivened throughout by his poetry and that of others, particularly Rilke and Blake.

The 'Iron John' of the title is a wild man covered with hair, discovered at the bottom of a lake by a lone hunter who has volunteered to investigate the disappearance of people in its vicinity. The hunter captures the wild man and hands him over to the king, who imprisons him in an iron cage in the castle courtyard. One day the king's young son is playing near the cage with a golden ball, which rolls inside the cage. The wild man offers to return it if the boy will release him and tells him the key is 145 hidden under his mother's pillow. The boy steals the key, releases the wild man and, now having compromised himself with his parents, sets off with him into the woods to begin his journey towards manhood.

This is just the first few pages of the story, which continues throughout the book. Bly uses it to illustrate his view of what is needed from men to complement the rich growth over the last twenty-five years in the roles and relationships of women. He is completely respectful of women's achievements and insistent that the new capacity of men for feeling and for sensitivity to women's needs must be preserved. But he believes that some powerful male energies with which we have lost touch, symbolised by Iron John, are needed, too.

The book needs to be read, I believe, not as a dry work of scholarship to be judged coolly by the mind, but as the work of a poet struggling to convey an emotional experience and leading us to what he has found within himself.

Don't Give a Man a Sword Until You Teach Him How to Dance

*I*n the ballroom of Gaunt's House, a country seat in Dorset devoted in recent years to the promulgation of 'new age' ideas and events concerned with psychological and spiritual growth, sixty men are shouting war-like chants at the top of their voices. They are lined up into two opposing sides, each two lines deep, and in time with the chanting each side in turn advances across the space between them, making the most threatening, insulting or obscene gestures they can think of. The fierce expressions on the faces are difficult to maintain, because they keep collapsing into laughter and it is clear that everyone is having a very good time.

This was the first evening of a weekend for men led by Robert Bly and Michael Meade, mythologist, story-teller and drummer, who has shared the leadership of the US men's movement with Bly and a number of others, including the Jungian analyst James Hillman and the trapper John Stokes. We had arrived two hours earlier, looked curiously at one another over dinner, and then taken chairs in the semicircles arranged around Bly and Meade for the opening session. Most adult males today, they said, remained boys because Western society has lost the tradition whereby older men take responsibility for ensuring that they become men. In more well-ordered societies the senior males would spend two-thirds of their time studying mythology, in order to initiate young males and help them access and handle the male energies responsible.

This began the input of mythological material. Men needed to pass through three stages in sequence: first, a period in which self-affirming and aggressive energies take centre stage; second, a time when altruistic concern for others prevails; and third, a painful, humbling stage where we become more human and balanced because these outwardly-directed energies give way to greater self-awareness and self-acceptance, where we see we have everything in us, good and bad, and accept our faults instead of blaming others. To make this journey we have to access a series of inner energies or instinctive patterns from which adverse early experience can sever us. One is the 'warrior' which enables us to recognise hostile attack and defend ourselves and our families from it. It is not the same as aggression, a point made by quoting the lively Celtic saying: 'Don't give a man a sword until you teach him how to dance.'

148   What is the evidence for all this? Certainly no

evidence of a scientific kind is offered, either in Bly's presentations or in his book, *Iron John*. There this sequence of unfolding energies is linked with certain events in the Grimms' fairy tale about the wild man of that name, who becomes a boy's guide towards true manhood. In the course of the story John enables the boy to fight and win three contests by providing him first with a red horse and armour, then white, and finally black, representing the three stages described above. As in the rest of the book, Bly draws upon his wide knowledge of mythology and symbolism to establish these psychological conclusions.

To the extent that I am able to use his ideas, they are not completely new to me. But by suggesting new relationships and connections among different separate facts, he enables me to see patterns and meanings unnoticed before.

The joke has it that psychiatrists go to the theatre to watch the audience. This certainly applies to me, and on the morning of the second day I took my place on one side of the half-circle where I had a good view of the whole gathering as well as of Bly and Meade. Looking around the room there was a subtle but unmistakable change in attitude, expressed in posture and bearing. People looked more alert and alive, with stronger voices, straighter backs, direct steady gaze and vigorous enjoyable male laughter. There was a powerful yet 149 quiet energy and attentiveness in the room that had not been there the night before.

The previous evening I had noticed one man in particular. He had been movingly open and honest about his inability to feel strongly, his over-attachment to his mother and his fear that he felt more female than male. His spine seemed collapsed, his whole bearing like an apology for his existence. In the 'war dance' he chanced to be opposite me; we caught each other's eye and I saw his enjoyment. This morning, as he related to the speakers, his bearing was completely different: more erect, self-affirming, relaxed, engaged and amused. What was causing these changes? There was no advice, encouragement or exhortation to be different, no pressure or political message. Some kind of different model was there to witness, men more comfortable with their manhood and enjoying it, but it was in no way imposed. Perhaps all we were getting was permission to be what we could always have been, something we had forgotten until we saw it.

What I was mainly experiencing was just good entertainment: amusing jokes and anecdotes; interesting conversation; poetry accompanied by drums and a stringed instrument; and, above all, marvellous stories. Stories teach by showing us people like ourselves getting it wrong, then gradu-
150 ally learning better. We see how they did it, how to

change if we wish to follow them. Our imagination is engaged and we are left free to use the knowledge as we wish, when we are ready, rather than being criticised and told we should be different. And the speakers, by sharing with us their own experience and exploration of what manhood is about, were themselves a living story leaving new questions and possibilities in our minds on which to ponder.

I am still questioning what I received at this gathering. It *feels* more than anything like a greater freedom from constraints on thought and feeling that previously were quite unconscious, thereby opening up new worlds of ideas and experience which promise to go on expanding.

Adjusting to Women

*W*hy have men been so slow in responding to the changes in women since women began to change so dramatically in the 1960s under the influence of the women's movement? In working professionally with families, I frequently found that the crucial problem was the father's reluctance to set clearer limits for the children. And working together with my late wife treating couples, the problem we met most often was a husband who was passively resisting and withdrawing emotionally from a wife who had been influenced by the changing roles of women and was becoming increasingly confident, independent and dissatisfied with him.

Of course, like everyone else I was also encountering the effect of these changes in my personal life. At first my wife was rather scornful of feminist ideas while I welcomed the idea of greater equality and sharing and in fact took the initiative in this direction. I even began cooking, despite encountering so much resistance that fighting my way into the kitchen was like landing on the Normandy beaches, and found myself liberated in the process from the power of a fantasy, true for babies but not for grown-ups, that you would die if a woman didn't feed you. Later she was influenced, like most other women, by the feminist ideas that were then in the air, and although there were periods of struggle and we found change was often painful for us both, I was never in doubt that the benefits far outweighed the losses, for men as for women.

In particular the release from feeling locked into the conventional male stereotype, tightly containing all but the more macho emotions, made possible a previously unimaginable openness, intimacy and warmth. And to my surprise, the more one accepted one's 'feminine' aspect, the more one enjoyed one's maleness as well. Since my bereavement, the process of mutual challenge and growth has continued with my new partner, a feminist who regularly attends a women's group, and I feel immensely grateful to be living at a time when relationships can be so much richer than the generation before me appeared to find them.

So, a satisfied customer myself, I am puzzled why it doesn't seem to be working for so many men who are younger than me. I have not understood why they feel uncertain about their male identity, why they can't enter into the game and enjoy the contest, why they don't find it fun. I don't mean arguing with militant extreme feminists, which is as uninteresting as arguing with Arthur Scargill about the merits of the Tory party, but just engaging in discussion with ordinary members of the opposite sex on an equal basis, and may the best human being win.

Then recently I was interviewed by David Thomas, former editor of *Punch*, for his book on men and feminism, *Not Guilty* (which I recommend highly), and found myself appearing to defend the male propensity for aggression and violence in a way that at first surprised me. But the more I thought about it, the more astonished I felt that I had not seen before what a central issue this is, and how it begins to explain the difficulty so many men have had in coming to terms with the way women have changed. It also explained why I had found it easier and more enjoyable myself; it was not *in spite of* being older, but *because of* being older.

What is a man? And what is a woman? Beyond certain inescapable biological facts we still really don't know because it is all changing so fast; except that both are similar in so many ways, and yet also different in vital respects that are extraordinarily hard to define. But only a woman can be the child-bearer and suckler, which the man can never be, and various other functions – childcare, homecare, cooking etc – followed naturally from that in the past even if they no longer necessarily do so. Various consequences arise from these biological facts for the man, too, and also from the high levels of male sex hormone which underlie his undisputed greater propensity for physical aggression and violence. Apart from his reproductive function of fertilising the egg, still essential though a fairly brief and simple matter, and now possible with even less of his participation through the technique of artificial insemination, throughout most of human history he has had at least two vital functions, both involving those capacities. First, as a hunter, killing animals to feed the family; and second, as a warrior, defending mother and children and the social group against aggressors. Violence is, or was, what he was for. Of course, it needs to be controlled and harnessed in the service of society; and regulating it was always the responsibility of the older men.

The development of Western culture and science has rendered both the latter male functions less necessary, or as easily, or better, performed by women. Nowadays the mighty hunter is probably less efficient than his spouse at tracking down the family bacon in Safeway or Tesco. And since the invention of the hydrogen bomb, which made a world war suicidal for everyone while the balance of terror held between the USA and the former Soviet Union, a woman could sit as easily as a man at the bottom of a missile silo ready to press the right buttons on receiving the command. Indeed, I would feel safer with a woman there. Since these changes, 155 and particularly since and because of the hydrogen bomb, a 'feminisation' of social values has taken place so gradually that I did not recognise it as such, and which I have seen advocated but not seen acknowledged as a reality. There are certain biological functions which are so different in the two sexes that one sex can never 'understand' the other in an emotional sense. Men cannot expect to feel the same about menstruation as women because it does not have the same significance in their lives. And women similarly are bound to be ambivalent about the male capacity for violence and to seek what is, in effect, their agreement to 'unilateral disarmament'. In recent times, no longer able to justify their capacity for physical aggression by the socially beneficial functions already mentioned, many younger men have disarmed and feel 'unmanned'.

I now see that I have been able to enjoy and benefit from the feminist challenge because I still also value and enjoy these male energies – as a result of active service as a pilot in the Second World War when the lives of families and the future of our country really were at stake, and appropriate violent response was rewarded by society. And also, because I believe the best new relationships will be found through the dialectic of engagement and contest between the sexes where each keeps its strengths, but seeks to learn from the other.

Catching Up on What You Missed

*P*sychotherapy is now acceptable in Britain, even becoming fashionable. But how many people know how it works? Essentially, all forms of psychotherapy have a similar goal: helping people to make good some important piece of social learning they missed at an earlier stage of life. When we are faced with a more responsible or complex job, we all accept that we may need to catch up or add to the subjects we studied at school by taking some further education. And similarly, facing new social situations like leaving home, getting married, bringing up children, and facing crises like redundancy, disappointment in love or bereavement, can make us aware that we lack some kind of understanding of ourselves or others, or some particular kind of strength or social skill.

Why should we be lacking in this way? It is usually something that our families or the communities we grew up in were not adequately able to give us. One person may have missed out on mothering because a younger sibling was seriously 157 ill and the mother was obliged to focus her main attention on this ailing child. The older child may suppress its emotional needs out of concern for their welfare, but then have difficulty expressing feelings and engaging robustly later on. Another person may have lacked a father who was serving abroad in the army during vital early years and so never learned, by having to share the mother with someone who has priority, to control his demands to have his own way in everything. Yet another may have lacked brothers and sisters, or playmates nearby, and had little practice in coping with the competitive rough and tumble of life. All these natural hazards can make relationships difficult in later life, or at least make them less enjoyable.

Normally, we tend to make good these deficiencies at some later stage by seeking out substitute mother and father figures, playmates, and other forms of social contact. We 'grow out' of our difficulties. But a very intense need for affection and support, normal in a young child and met readily by its parents, is not usually welcomed by others when expressed by an adult. Even in marriage, where these early needs can most often be remedied, there are limits to what one partner can give without receiving something in return. And when the missing experience cannot be found in ordinary life, the necessary learning, or unlearning and relearning, will need a special situation guided by a

158

professional with the necessary knowledge, skill, and patience. The behaviour therapies, like 'social skills training' and 'Masters and Johnson' type sex therapy based on practical methods, have their greatest value here together with many forms of counselling.

But there are two major complications. First of all, for this substitute learning to be possible a person must be aware of the deficiency. But if, as a child, his parents found it hard to acknowledge their own limitations and became upset or angry when his behaviour made them aware of them, this awareness may be lost. His demanding behaviour may reflect their own selfishness, for instance, or his tantrums may remind them of their own irritability. The resulting disapproval and rejection may then lead the child to hide these expressions of his inner feelings and ultimately, since he knows the parents would reject him if they were aware of his true feelings, to suppress and hide them even from himself. Once this has happened, the deprivation still undermines the person's ability to function well, but the reason is no longer clear. It is as if someone has suppressed his knowledge of the law of gravity, keeps walking over cliffs and wonders why he goes on hurting himself. Instead, the missing social learning now presents to the doctor as 'nervous symptoms' – depression, anxiety, phobias or whatever.

One of my first patients, for example, suffered   159

from intense migraine headaches and an 'engagement neurosis' – increasing anxiety at the prospect of permanent commitment. My suspicion that he had repressed his anger in childhood was rapidly confirmed as, in treatment, the migraines were replaced by rages, which then came under control and, as he became confident that he could 'stand his ground' with his fiancée, a loss of his fear of close involvement. Where a person has learned in this way to hide his problems even from himself, then before the missing experience can be provided and made up the patient first has to get in touch with the suppressed need. The therapist must be familiar with the many ways in which deficiencies in learning can be hidden and disguised. Some understanding is desirable of dreams and symbolism in general, together with a sensitivity for the subtle changes in direction that take place in conversation when hidden emotions are approached and avoided. The therapist also has to recognise the ways in which the underlying difficulties can be incorporated in a particular type of personality which can be seen as positive, in which case it is then called a 'character disorder'. A person who has suppressed and denied his normal aggression and no longer has it available for constructive use may, for example, vent that anger in support of pacifism, animal rights or other

worthy causes, through violence and intimidation

rather than for better reasons in a democratic and peaceful way.

A second complication arises when the already suppressed problems interfere with a constructive relationship in the therapy itself. For example, patients who have protected themselves against hurt in childhood by withdrawing and distrusting others, may distrust the therapist and withdraw there, too. Or someone whose father shrank from exerting his authority may subsequently defy and provoke conflicts with bosses and other authority figures and block progress in the therapy by the same stubbornly argumentative attitude. In such cases the therapist needs not only to trace the hidden source of the deprivation, and help to remedy it, but first of all must know how to recognise and circumvent the obstacles to communication that the problem causes in the interview itself.

Fortunately this is by far the most effective way both to understand and change the underlying difficulties – in the here-and-now of the exchange between therapist and patient rather than in discussions about memories from the past. The knowledge available from psychoanalysis, group analysis and their derivatives comes into its own here, and often make treatment possible when other methods fail.

Nevertheless, what I have said above is too cut   161

and dried. Although different types of treatment are in general more appropriate to different kinds of problem, the two complications mentioned are encountered in most cases at least to some extent. The best therapists will therefore be equipped with some understanding and skill related to all three levels even if they concentrate mainly on one of them. Fortunately, this training in a wide spectrum of treatment methods is increasingly seen among training programmes today.

The Hazards of Therapy

D ifferent types of problem need different types of therapy. First, a more behavioural or educational approach is appropriate where a person is still aware of the underlying causes; second, a more exploratory and uncovering method where past sufferings and problematic emotions have been buried and lost from memory; and third, more complex techniques focused mainly on the emotions felt by the patient and therapist towards one another when these get in the way of both the above more simple approaches. But unfortunately this choice of the best kind of therapy, and then of a therapist with whom a good collaboration is possible, is the most crucial and difficult part of the whole treatment.

The decision is complicated first of all by natural anxieties about where the process is going to lead. One of the commonest fears is that, once started, it will be impossible ever to stop. If we have missed out on some good experience in the family we grew up in and covered the deficiency over in a way that 163 enables us at least to cope with life, the idea of actually getting what we were deprived of can arouse fears of becoming hopelessly addicted, so enslaved by the re-awakened needs that we might want to return permanently to the enjoyment of our lost childhood and so lose our hard-won adulthood and independence.

This fear is natural, precisely because the nature and intensity of the buried feelings are unknown. The whole reason why they have continued to restrict our enjoyment of life, or diminished our capacity for successful work and relationships, is that we have not satisfied and thereby outgrown the needs at an earlier stage. To contemplate satisfying them now feels in some ways attractive, but also scary and embarrassing. We behave like a starving person who has suppressed the hunger-pangs and got used to going without food, who is at last confronted with a good dinner and hesitates to eat it for fear it will be too enjoyable and arouse the desire to have dinners regularly. Provided there is plenty of food available the idea is ridiculous. But to someone who has grown up in a world where there was never enough there is also a kind of logic in this response.

For such a person the danger of trust was once real, the fear of enjoyment justified. Braving the experience of the fear in a situation where it is no longer justified, by exposing oneself to therapy, is then the main part of the cure. Far from being a prelude after which the real therapy can start, this anxiety over becoming involved in therapy at all is usually the most crucial part of the process, and the fear and uncertainty will be encountered repeatedly in one form or another as it is faced more squarely, until it gradually wanes to be replaced by confidence and trust. For instance, anxiety about commitment may recur each time a holiday break in the treatment is imminent, and when the therapist is less attentive through illness or some other distraction. It usually returns intensely as the end of the treatment draws near, and seeing this through to an agreed date, without escaping by an abrupt more comfortable parting, probably brings more benefit eventually than all the treatment that went before. The inner struggle about whether to engage in treatment or to continue it once started is thus the central question around which the obstacles to love and trust are most vividly experienced and changed.

What I have said so far has focused on the resources and limitations of the patient. But what about the therapist? The patient's problems of deprivation have usually developed in a family where the parents were themselves deprived, and therefore too needy of their children's support to be able either to give them a sense of security and confidence, or to let them go to get the love and   165 support somewhere else. People from this kind of family background have every reason to fear that an encounter with therapy might repeat the original failure, leaving them not only more disappointed and distrustful than ever, but even more vulnerable through having let down their guard, sacrificing the relative safety of their previous isolation.

Unfortunately, this kind of failure does happen. Occasionally it is due to incompetence or unprofessional behaviour, and the more extreme cases where therapists have broken the trust laid upon them by entering into a physical sexual relationship during the course of therapy has recently been a focus of books and newspaper articles – in the US one study reported that over six per cent of therapists *admitted* breaking the boundaries in this manner! But here the failure is obvious, the betrayal of trust can be seen for what it is, and the treatment is likely soon to be broken off. Perhaps more harmful in some ways – in my opinion at least – are therapists who are covertly gratifying their own needs for emotional intimacy through their contacts with patients, as a substitute for real involvement and commitment elsewhere on a mutual basis. Paradoxically, this does not necessarily impair the therapy if therapists are aware of the problem in themselves and are struggling with it, just as children are spared from taking on those psycho-logical problems of their parents that the parents see

166

and are facing squarely, whether they have solved them or not. Indeed, I believe that this type of relationship difficulty is what attracts most therapists to their work in the first place; that it mirrors the pattern of their families of origin; and that when they see their own predicament and its similarity to that of their patients, it not only helps them to understand and overcome the problem in themselves but makes them exceptionally good at helping others do the same.

On the other hand, therapists who do not recognise this truth about themselves will end up vicariously gratifying their own needs by projecting them into, and 'helping', others. I have called this the 'Me Tarzan, mature competent therapist; you Jane, helpless needy patient' syndrome. In this game of 'doctors and patients' the therapist agrees to play the grown-up role and take responsibility for looking after both, as long as the patient plays out the role of the dependent child for the therapist as well. When this happens, both feel better as long as the treatment continues, but threatened by an ending to the therapy, where each would either lose the half of themselves invested in the other, or be faced again with the problems they began with. Small wonder that the six-month analyses of Freud's day have lengthened to two, three, five, ten, and now sometimes over twenty years.

The Therapist's Role in Change

When one brings the whole family together for therapy problems can often be solved very quickly, sometimes in a single interview. But when the process is examined in detail one sees that the changes brought about by the treatment are very small, though the effect when multiplied over time may be great. I often wonder whether I do anything more, in my work with couples, than introduce a small delay into the conversation just by the fact that I don't understand the underlying reasons for their arguments and interrupt from time to time to ask a question. I used to think when they achieved a happier relationship that it was my brilliant unearthing of these underlying dynamics that did the trick. No doubt such understanding helps, but I am now inclined to think that it is more my expression of mystification and bewilderment, and repeated raising of a hand with interjections of 'Hang on! Hang on! Whatever did you mean by that?'

A major contribution to most marital altercations 168 is the failure of partners simply to listen to one another. Each hears the first bit of what the other is saying, senses criticism, and goes off at half-cock without listening to the full message which might have been quite reasonable. When two people do this an accelerating chain-reaction develops, ending in a large explosion. So the introduction of an interested and curious but sufficiently stupid or sleepy third party like myself may just be having a similar effect to those tiresome sleeping policemen which are spreading like a skin disease along the local roads, slowing things down a bit and so reducing the collisions.

After a few of these gruelling experiences of trying to help me understand what's going on, I think couples discover that, if they simply hear the partner out before replying, the complaints expressed are not always unreasonable and may even have some justice. And once they discover this in the interviews they have reason to sustain the slower tempo and the greater warmth and co-operation it brings for increasing periods of time in between, until it becomes as much a habit as the touchy explosiveness was before.

What I am speaking about is not at all the same as trying to be nice, trying to be tolerant, and certainly not listening with a martyred expression, using the time to compose a scorching reply. It means genuinely suspending one's own response and giving full attention to the partner with both one's eyes and ears, as well as bringing real thought and self-questioning to what they say and feel. This is the model I think I provide in the interview – easy enough for me, of course, since I am not personally involved and suffering as they are.

Another consequence of being listened to in this way is that one can have that rare experience of listening to *oneself*, something one is protected from when the partner reacts immediately. Really hearing what one says can be a shock, and this is another vital curative factor in such interviews. It is not so much the clever comments or interpretations of the therapist that strike home and have a deep effect, as the sobering realisation by the person speaking, when his or her view of the problem is slowly clarified by detailed examples, that it just does not make sense or at least is one-sided and unfair. To realise this about oneself has a far more profound and enduring effect than being told the same thing by someone else, even by a neutral party. Delaying the interaction also does not mean trying to agree, or even trying to like one another. What it does mean is providing conditions which make it more possible to reach the truth, however unpleasant that may be. Real listening, suspending knee-jerk emotional responses, has to be sustained despite periods when painful things are said, words which had previously led the participants to withdraw, close off emotionally, and become defensive, thus preventing any further communication.

The possibility that much marital harmony and happiness depends on such simple, practical factors is reassuring to most people, which is why I mention it here. Sustaining the honest exchange of negative feelings may sometimes require the safety provided by the presence of a third party. But anyone can try honestly listening to their partner, any time they like, and we all can only gain by it.

This kind of discovery, that many successes in one's chosen work are brought about by very simple factors, easily understood by anyone, rather than through painfully acquired professional knowledge, probably has to wait until one is old enough not to be worried about playing a humbler role than one envisaged at medical school. And there is the compensation of finding that, as with the 'good-enough' mother, even one's personal failures can sometimes bring about positive changes.

At the beginning of a first interview with a very defensive couple, the strains of 'Colonel Bogey' interrupted our strained conversation. Startled, it took me some seconds before I realised it was the alarm of the cheap waterproof watch I use for windsurfing which was in my briefcase. Once located, I realised I did not know how to turn it off, so we all had to sit and listen to it for the full minute the alarm played. I thought the interview was 171 disrupted but to my surprise the ice was broken and an unusually constructive interview followed.

Another couple had been referred by a distin-guished colleague whose letter indicated that the relationship was difficult and that they were very doubtful about the whole idea of marital therapy. They were indeed prickly and guarded, and as I began the interview, taking down the usual routine details about ages, occupations, children and so on, I feared that I would not succeed in winning their confidence. After about five minutes one of them said, 'You did take all this information last week, you know.' I had been unusually distracted around that time by family illness and realised, to my consternation, that I had indeed seen them for a first interview the week before. At first I assumed I had totally blown it and that, besides losing them, my reputation with the referring colleague would do a nose-dive. But they had now relaxed and lost their defensiveness. Instead they were amused and friendly, putting me at my ease and establishing a trusting relationship which led to useful work. As I showed them to the door they both grinned as one said, 'Next time we'll both wear false beards!'

Who Do the Helping Services Help?

A remarkable gathering recently took place at the Wembley Conference Centre. Delegates from all over Europe, including almost every newly-liberated country formerly behind the Iron Curtain and from Russia itself, joined with Western colleagues to review the present state of the family and assess the great range of methods now available to help with family problems. Opened by among others Lord Ennals and Lord Justice Butler-Sloss, it was organised by the Institute of Family Therapy, London, together with its associated charity, Familes At Risk, which gave its name for the title of the conference.

Why remarkable? It is difficult to pinpoint exactly why it was such a good experience, though I ended the week feeling the world was a better place. Certainly one factor was the presence of the East Europeans because it was so inspiring to be among these people, whose hardships one reads about and sees on television every day, and yet to find them not in the least despondent or subdued as one 173 might expect, but an example to us all in their cheerfulness, warmth and generosity of spirit. Their presence was also a powerful factor in bringing the rest of us back to the roots of our own early interest in working with families. Still enthralled by the wonder of what families can accomplish just with the stimulus of a therapist's simple directness and curiosity, and not yet sophisticated enough to become intoxicated with jargon, fail to see the wood for the trees, or the family for the video cameras and team behind the one-way screen, they put us in touch again with experiences that had first attracted us to our chosen work.

This return to basics was in any case built into the discussions. Each day dealt with a different family theme: changes in marriage and the roles of men and women, including patterns of divorce; marriage and step-parenting; issues of race and culture; violence and abuse; promotion of mental health in the community; and throughout the whole event the central questions of the influence of changing family patterns on society and how social policy could help the family.

For my own presentation I looked back over my own experience – thirty years of seeing families together – and reflected on the way our understanding and treatment of family problems had developed. I had been struck by what seemed an inevitable sequence whereby family therapy, like

174

psychoanalysis and other forms of treatment before it, had at the same time made great advances in knowledge and technical skills, yet lost something vital and in some ways become less effective in the process. The more I considered it, the more widely this pattern seemed to apply. All the 'helping services', as we call them, begin with the aim of serving the needs of their clients. And in their early stages they do so. They have their origin when some person or group recognises an unmet social need, or becomes dissatisfied with existing methods of treatment and searches for a solution. At this stage no one *knows*; everyone knows they don't know, and everyone is happy to learn from everyone else. Having as yet no place in the existing professional structure and no landmarks to guide them in the new territory they are exploring, there is among the pioneers a wonderful sense of comradeship and mutual support, of excitement, and of openness to new ideas and experience even if they contradict accepted doctrines. There are no problems about who will be king of the castle because there is, as yet, no castle to be king of. Above all, the aim is to find new ways to help their clients, and the central value is a search for truth.

However, all this begins to change with success, when the new profession is accepted and becomes established. Now there is something to lose and inevitably the central aim turns towards 175 preservation of what has been accomplished. The earlier attitudes of openness and exploration gradually change towards conformity and defence of existing ideas, backed now by a different kind of research where we become more and more sure about details it is less and less useful to know. As soon as the new profession offers status, money, a career, increasing numbers want to climb aboard the band-wagon. Training requirements and qualifications bring barriers restricting entry, where those fortunate enough to get in have to demonstrate that they know, and can successfully put into practice, the accepted current theories and techniques. In the growing anxiety to demonstrate therapeutic 'success' the concern moves imperceptibly towards what we can do *to* families, and away from what they really want and need *from* us. Not only do we lose sight of the original aim to serve our patients and clients, we also forget the obligation to see our place in, and to serve, the wider professional and social systems of which we form part. Not least, we neglect to study ourselves and our own motivation, and so confuse our clients' agenda with our own.

As this happens, the service increasingly comes to serve the needs of the professionals, rather than the clients. In the hospital out-patient department, a roomful of people may wait for hours for fear the consultant might occasionally wait a few minutes.

176

And though psychiatric departments usually run appointments systems, too often everyone who comes through the door is forced into a Procrustean bed of drug treatment, or analytic psychotherapy, or behaviour therapy, or family therapy, or whatever the latest local fashion may be. Those who don't or won't fit are judged 'unsuitable for treatment' or 'uncooperative'. In individual psychotherapy, at least when carried out by men, the ideal patient becomes a woman who is beautiful, young, intelligent and mentally healthy, while the 'normal' duration of treatment rises from six months to two years, to five years, to ten years, until you wonder who the sessions are for.

I had feared that my presentation might be unwelcome. But, as often happens, the ideas seemed already to be there and were echoed many times in the exchanges that followed, becoming at the end almost a central theme. I began to see that openness, concern for truth and real care of families have, like liberty, to be fought for all the time if we are not to lose them. The conference gave evidence that this battle was at the moment going well.

Family Therapist as Family Scapegoat

Much of my work as a psychotherapist in the individual and group treatment of adults, children and families in the sixties and seventies was carried out in the most severely deprived areas of the East End of London, with unusually high rates of delinquency, psychosis, multi-problem families etc. It became clear to my colleagues and myself very early on that the neutral, analytic position from which we originally tried to operate, which was positively experienced by our middle-class patients as a form of respect for their freedom and independence, was experienced quite differently by the disadvantaged. The more severely deprived and disturbed seemed to feel this as a lack of caring on our part, a lack of interest in their welfare, a refusal to offer them some more effective mode of functioning, which our higher economic status suggested to them we possessed, in place of the inadequate one they were using already, which our interpretations seemed only to shatter and leave in greater ruin than before.

178   We found, like many other workers had done

before in similar situations, that in these cases the therapist has to go beyond recognising and describing what he perceives as missing or distorted. He actually has to provide what is missing in the individual or family, or to correct what is distorted, through his intervention. He must be actively involved, and seen to be involved and concerned, providing an input designed to change the families functioning in a direction he believes, to the best of his judgement, to be in their interests.

The great advantage of interventions based on this type of 'modelling', as it is often termed, is that the effects, when they are successful, are often immediate, or at least exceedingly rapid. If one provides an input of forceful control to a family where the problems are all stemming from absence of clear structure and hierarchy, changes in the family functioning can be noticed during the interview itself, with subsequent increasingly heated exchanges showing mounting anger inhibited by mounting anxiety, culminating in an explosion where a parent 'reads the riot act', a clear hierarchy is finally established and conflict and anxiety suddenly drop.

The disadvantage of this is that the therapist has to take over responsibility for the patient's life to a certain extent, and is in a sense imposing his values, which may of course be unhealthy or prejudiced. People who make modelling interventions exclusively tend to develop theories and techniques which are applied rigidly and uncritically, limiting the further development of the theories. And since criticism is not two-way, the personality and behaviour of the therapist do not come under scrutiny, and while inputs are received by the patients to improve their functioning, the therapists do not receive inputs from the patients which would improve theirs.

I think the essence of my own technique is that I, as therapist, voluntarily and actively undertake the scapegoat role. I do not distance myself from the family emotions, but at first allow myself to be open and receptive to them. Gradually I become part of the family system and begin to feel, without being able to explain it, strong impulses of one sort or another. I may feel pain at their emotional isolation, anger at the chaos and disruption, or irritated by their prudishness and impelled to make some provocative sexual remark.

Instead of describing what is missing I actually *become* what is missing. The emotions the family cannot deal with begin to happen in their midst, in the actual person to whom they have come to save them from this dreaded experience, and short of escaping through the door they have to cope with them somehow. Seen in this way the situation is so horrifying, so shocking that one might be surprised if something dramatic didn't happen!

During the course of a workshop which my wife, Prudence, and I once made on a trip to Nova Scotia, we were asked to see a Canadian family which had just begun in treatment at a local clinic, to give a demonstration interview on closed-circuit television. This interview gave an unusually clear illustration of the principles set out above, and in addition demonstrated the rich personal benefits which can accrue from this way of working.

The family comprised four children between the ages of eleven and three, two adopted and two 'natural', together with the parents who both attended. The mother, who appeared a pleasant, effective and competent person, did most of the talking and described the problem – stealing in the second eldest, one of the natural children. The father was courteous and co-operative, but had little to say; indeed, there seemed little opportunity for him to add anything to his wife's very effective account.

Prudence, who shared the co-therapy task with me, conducted her part of the interview with striking confidence and effectiveness, which I greatly admired. I found it difficult to think of anything to add, and found myself playing with the baby, whose sex I kept mistaking, and receiving presents of pictures from the other children where I repeatedly became confused as to which were the natural children, and which were adopted.

After about twenty minutes of this, I commented that there seemed to be no place for me in the interview because my wife was being so effective, and   181

I related this to the difficulty the father seemed to be experiencing in contributing when his wife was so competent. The father identified with this comment, and obviously felt supported; although he had been somewhat resistant in earlier interviews at the clinic, it was reported later that he had left the session 'walking on air'.

My wife commented on the feeling of deprivation in the family, saying that her impulse was to pick the referred patient up and cuddle her. I said that I had felt a similar feeling towards the mother, as if her competent exterior covered strong needs for support and affection that she could not reveal to her husband for fear of disappointment. The mother confirmed that this was true, and was able to reveal that she had resembled the referred patient as a child.

The interview seemed to be effective in opening up dynamic patterns which had not previously been apparent to the professionals dealing with the case. But the interest in the present context lies in the way in which my wife and I quickly began to mirror the family dynamics in our co-therapy relationship. My ability to sustain an excluded, incompetent role (which extended even to letting the interview overrun the videotape, a mistake I had never made before) and my wife's ability to be over-competent and exclude me, provided the vital information which gave the key to the underlying parental dynamics. This quickly reached the mother's feelings of deprivation, and enabled me to support the father in perhaps the only way possible without diminishing him.

Following the interview, my wife was quite withdrawn and depressed, and this mood continued well into the next day. I am usually intolerant and attacking when this occurs, feeling that she has deserted me at a time when I most need her support, but the family interview had given me a new understanding of our own relationship, which changed my behaviour and enabled me to perceive her need for me to be supportive and accepting. This enabled her, in turn, to go through the depression and to face, constructively, a feeling of inadequacy which underlay it. Later in the visit, when she had recovered and I was beginning to experience the anxiety I always feel as endings and departures approach, I was able to reveal this to her more easily and her ability to know this and keep me company in it, rather than to withdraw or to support me, was a good experience.

The incident, which put us both in touch more deeply with early deprivation experiences, demonstrates unusually clearly how the resonance of the therapists' emotions to those of the family not only provides the most effective point of intervention therapeutically, but often enables the therapists to gain better understanding and resolution of their personal problems.

Getting Our Own Act Together

O ne of the biggest difficulties in bringing up children, or for that matter trying to further the process of one's own growing-up, is judging whether anyone is getting better or getting worse. Long-term improvement in our functioning often requires an unleashing of inhibited energies, which to start with are difficult to manage and feel dangerous and a threat to our relationships.

One of my first patients was referred for treatment of an 'engagement neurosis', a fear of commitment and an impulse to escape as his wedding day approached. He also suffered from severe migraines and a phobia of violence. As he rediscovered his long-repressed rage, in the primitive form in which it had been buried early in childhood, his headaches diminished and disappeared. Able now to stand up for himself and say 'no' to unreasonable demands, he also lost his fear of engulfment and was able to marry. But his buried anger was at first terrifying him to the point of fearing he might commit murder.

Couples in joint therapy often experience similar anxieties as deeper emotions come to the surface which they fear may lead to a break-up. But groups composed of couples are extraordinarily effective at containing and controlling violent feelings safely. It is a pity they are not used more.

Of course, one has to feel comfortable about weathering such storms oneself before one dares to work with a couples' group at all, and this is probably what holds people back from attempting them. My late wife, Prue, and I did not begin until quite late in life, around fifty, when we felt we were ready. How did we know we were ready? I can remember vividly the experience which made us confident that we could expose ourselves to the marital tensions of others. I have already reported it to a meeting of the Royal College of Psychiatrists and may as well record it again now.

About twenty years ago, when our children were around eight and ten, Prue asked me to take them all for one of those happy Saturday afternoons at the movies. I agreed in order to show I was a good father since my occupation at that time as a consultant child psychiatrist made it difficult to deny that good fathers should take part in family outings. But it was one of the worse Walt Disney whimsies, which I dislike. So I went with a bad grace and as soon as it was over, which couldn't have been soon enough for me, we piled into the car to return home. 185

On the way, the children in the back seat asked for ice-creams. I was looking forward to a stiff whisky as soon as we got inside the door, but before I could even have a chance to show I was a good father again, Prue told me the children wanted ice-creams, and would I stop. With a screech of brakes we drew up at the ice-cream shop, Prue got out, leaned back into the car, and said 'That's three cornets then?'

I said, 'What d'you mean, *three* cornets! Why can't *I* have a cornet? I've come with you all to the pictures; why am I the only one who doesn't get an ice-cream?'

Prue behaved with admirable restraint and refused to be provoked. She just said, 'All right, *four* cornets then', and went off to get them. When she returned she handed a cornet each to the children in the back seat, gave one to me, got back in the car holding hers, and shut her door ready for us to drive off again. Just as I was about to let in the clutch to do so, my ice-cream fell off the top of my cone onto the floor. Now if you have, or have had, children, you will know that at this stage of life the floors of cars are covered with sand and grass. Prue said, 'Your ice-cream has fallen on the floor', helpless with amusement.

'I know my ice-cream is on the floor,' I replied. 'Pick it up and put it back on my cone.' The whole family were now convulsed with laughter.

'But it's got grass and sand all over it,' she said.

'I know it's got grass and sand all over it,' I replied. 'I'm not blind. Please pick it up, scrape the grass off, and put it back on again.'

'But I've only got one hand; I'm holding my own cornet.'

'*I'll* hold your cornet, now pick up my ice-cream and give it back to me,' I repeated. I took her cornet in one hand and held out my empty cone with the other, waiting for her to replace my refurbished but shrunken ice-cream on the top. Eventually she had it reasonably clean, took the empty cone from my hand, and began to press it firmly down. But she took her time over it and laughed once too often. It was a summer evening so the car windows were down, and I threw *her* ice-cream out of the window on my side.

She said, 'Oh, all right then!' and flung *my* ice-cream out of *her* window. I let in the clutch and we sped home, both now laughing and in the most excellent spirits, my bad mood completely gone, having achieved the first really 'good clean row' of our relationship. A bit late in the day, you may say, and of course you're right; but some of us take longer than others, and better late than never. Anyway, we later realised that this was the change that signalled our readiness to collaborate as co-therapists with groups of couples, which we found stimulating and fun for the rest of our life together.

In the car there was silence from the back seat for

a few moments, and then my heart sank and my enjoyment of our new emotional freedom vanished as I heard our son say *'Daddy!'* in a reproving, anguished tone. I suddenly became aware of how this episode might appear to those looking on. We were in NW3, psychoanalyst country; suppose there had been one passing by, or a member of the Royal College of Psychiatrists or the Association of Child Psychology and Psychiatry, speculating on the damage I was doing to our hapless children? Perhaps we had even hit this innocent bystander with one of the ice-creams. However, I was quickly reassured as our son added, 'Daddy! don't you realise those cornets cost a *shilling each!*'

A Recipe for Health and Happiness

*I*n 1988, I drove to Cornwall for a family marriage and visited the place where I was born, a tiny village and port preserved almost exactly as it was two hundred years ago. My wife had died about six months earlier, an event which naturally brought great grief, but which, to my surprise, was combined with a kind of joy at the good relationship we had had. So I suppose I was in a heightened emotional state and more receptive to events, and that may have had something to do with the experience that followed.

I walked about, looking at the house where I was born, the beach, harbour, cliffs and fields where I spent so much of my childhood. It was a brilliant sunny day with a light breeze. As I walked out on to the quay, I thought what a marvellous place it must be for someone to grow up – how no-one growing up here could fail to have a happy childhood.

Then I remembered that I had had an extremely *unhappy* childhood. But it was too late: my memories of it were already changing. It is hard to describe what happened, but it was as if a series of photographs was being flipped over rapidly, so that I saw the pictures differently.

What I was realising was that I had been blessed with experiences which, despite many problems and deficiencies, could have been responded to with enjoyment, love and gratitude. But for various reasons I had chosen to react with disappointment, resentment and withdrawal. Since that time this extraordinary revision of my memory has remained, to my surprise and pleasure, in its updated, more cheerful form.

As I was over sixty-five at the time it happened, my experience shows that profound change is possible at any time of life, supporting the aphorism, 'It is never too late to have a happy childhood.' This implies something more important: whatever the cause of mental health and ill-health, happiness and unhappiness, we are not necessarily stuck at a level fixed in childhood, but can move up and down the scale.

Although this sudden change came out of the blue, it was part of a process which had been going on ever since I began trying to understand myself better at the beginning of my teens. During my childhood and youth I experienced a wide range of the kind of emotional behavioural and psychosomatic problems which I later came to treat in children referred to my child guidance clinics, without being able to understand why or being able

190

to escape. I spent the next forty years looking for some guide which would explain me to myself and make sense of the behaviour of people around me. I began to read philosophy and psychology but found little that helped. And when I took up medicine and psychiatry, I scoured the library at the Institute of Psychiatry for articles and books on health, but found just three articles – and only one contained anything useful. Eventually, I took up the study of families, searching for what it was that made the difference between mental health and mental ill-health, happiness and unhappiness. I became more and more excited as, gradually, some basic principles began to emerge.

When these findings were sufficiently clear, I put them in my first book, *One Flesh: Separate Persons*. By chance, this book was published in the US at the same time as the first study of exceptionally healthy families. Researchers had compared these exceptionally healthy families with unhealthy families showing severe mental illness in some members, and also with average families – the kind to which most of us belong. I couldn't put the book down because the findings were so similar to my own conclusions, even though I never saw exceptionally healthy families at my clinics but had guessed what they might be like.

The results of the healthy family research seem almost common sense. A lot of what goes to make a healthy family describes how we all behave in our better moments, when we are in a good mood, when things are going well, and when we know we are behaving honourably and responsibly, when we feel loved and valued for ourselves.

The exceptionally healthy families are characterised by a high level of humour, fun and enjoyment. The research team describes watching them as 'like watching a three-ring circus – many things happening at once but somehow all under control'. There are several features which make this possible: the first – and most important – is that they have a basically positive attitude and are warm, friendly, concerned, kind and supportive towards others, both inside and outside the family, and play a responsible and respected part in the communities they live in. At the other end of the scale – in chaotic families showing extremes of mental disorder – there are tendencies towards hostility, distrust, and paranoia, or social withdrawal and isolation.

In the average or 'normal' family, the members may be basically responsible and decent, but there is not the same feeling of security, enjoyment and freedom. You tend to find more anxiety over losing out or not getting enough, which can range from exploitation and manipulation of others, through 'What's in it for me?' or 'I'm all right, Jack' attitudes, to clinging, possessive relationships where each partner worries about whether they're getting as much out as they're putting in. Of course, generosity and openness will always arouse warmth and trust in others, while suspicion, meanness and withdrawal will merely arouse guardedness and distance. So the attitudes typical of each level of health are self-fulfilling: we all end up living in the kind of world we expect. We don't realise that we can move to a better world at any time we like because we don't realise that we are *creating* the one we live in. The same applies to how we feel about ourselves and our inner worlds, which is why it was possible for me to be living in one world as I walked out along the quay in my home village, and in another world when I walked back.

The second most important feature is more of a surprise. In the most healthy families, people seem able to be extremely committed, intimate and involved, and show a pattern of long-term fidelity. But they are also able to alternate between that and being separate, independent and happy on their own. They do not 'need' each other in the way that, at its extreme, makes us say, 'I can't live without you' or 'You are my life.' But because of this capacity for separateness, the relationship can be based on mutual liking and enjoyment. The partner – and children – are respected and enjoyed for what they are, without any attempt to force them into a mould or load them with expectations and demands.

The third difference is in communication. At the unhealthy end of the scale, the communication is confused, contradictory and evasive. Most healthy families, however, talk to one another in a way that is open, clear, direct and frank; giving and getting accurate information.

The fourth and fifth points were reassuring to me. We live in a time when there has been much controversy about the amount of authority that parents should use but, in my work in child guidance, I found that restoring the confidence of parents to exercise firmness often quickly resolved problems that had not responded to months of conventional psychotherapy. The research supported this, and showed that the healthiest parents had no inhibition about taking an authoritative role when this was required, although they would always consult the children and reach a democratic decision as far as possible. In the most healthy families, the father and the mother were able to share power easily and amicably – in contrast to the unhealthy families where the parents were unable to cooperate. They also differed from the average family which showed a more rigid hierarchy with one or other parent assuming a dominant position.

The most unhealthy families were found to swing between extremes of emotions, without being aware of the inconsistency, and their general atmos-
194 phere was a negative one. In the average family,

feelings such as anger, jealousy and sadness were repressed within the family while being condemned when expressed by others. This leads to an over-controlled, low-key and joyless emotional life. In the most healthy families, however, *all* feelings were accepted as natural – although people were expected to learn to control them – and the overall emotional tone was warm and positive.

Finally, the differences in the families' abilities to cope with change and loss – including the death of a loved one – were striking. The reason for this seemed to be the support provided by the other members of the family, the wide social network of which these families were valued members and the family's sense of meaning and purpose, which came from a 'transcendent value system' of some kind. This is often a formal religion, but could also be a humanitarian philosophy that gives meaning to life.

Of course, creating a healthy and happy family is more easily said than done. At the same time, if we are hopelessly lost it can make all the difference to have pointers which help us discover where we are, and the direction in which we need to travel to reach our destination.